THE GOSPEL OF
MARY
MAGDALENE

Also by Jean-Yves Leloup

The Gospel of Philip
The Gospel of Thomas
The Sacred Embrace of Jesus and Mary

THE GOSPEL OF
MARY
MAGDALENE

Translation from the Coptic and Commentary by Jean-Yves Leloup

*English Translation and
Notes by Joseph Rowe*

Inner Traditions
Rochester, Vermont

Inner Traditions International
One Park Street
Rochester, Vermont 05767
www.InnerTraditions.com

First U.S. edition published by Inner Traditions in 2002

Originally published in French under the title *L'Évangile de Marie: Myriam de Magdala* by Albin Michel

LIBRARY OF CONGRESS CATALOGING-IN-PUBLICATION DATA

Evangile de Marie. English & Coptic.
The gospel of Mary Magdalene / Coptic translation and commentary by Jean-Yves Leloup ; English translation and notes by Joseph Rowe ; preface by Jacob Needleman.—1st U.S. ed.
p. cm.
Includes bibliographical references.
ISBN 978-0-89281-911-9 (pbk.)
1. Gospel of Mary—Commentaries. 2. Gnosticism. I. Leloup, Jean-Yves. II. Rowe, Joseph, 1942– III. Title.
BT1392.G65 A3 2001
229' .8—dc21

2001006735

Printed and bound in the United States by Lake Book Manufacturing, Inc.

22

Text design and layout by Virginia Scott Bowman
This book was typeset in Caslon with Copperplate as the display typeface

CONTENTS

FOREWORD

The Gospel of Mary first came to light in Cairo in 1896, some fifty years before the revolutionary discovery in Nag Hammadi, Egypt, of what have come to be known as the Gnostic gospels, the most well-known of which is the Gospel of Thomas. Like them, the Gospel of Mary offers the modern man or woman a new perception of the immensity of Christianity and the figure of Jesus.

It is clear that in both root and essence the teaching of Jesus is a vision and a *way* that has been given to mankind from a source far above our known qualities of mind and sensibility. The luminosity and mystery of what he said and did two thousand years ago is a "shock from above" that changed the world and that continues to reverberate in the hopes of millions over the whole face of the earth. But the inner and outer conditions of modern life are such that it has become nearly impossible for many of us to *hear* the spiritual traditions of the world. The Gospel of Mary, taken with the inspired commentary by Jean-Yves Leloup, can help toward making the teaching of Jesus once again alive—that is, *unknown,* not in the negative sense, but in the great and fertile meaning of that word.

Every spiritual teaching sounds a call from above. But, as the present text announces and demonstrates, the central aim of the teaching of Jesus is to sensitize us to the *above* that also calls to us from within ourselves. The immensity of Christianity takes its interior meaning as a sign of an immensity within the self of every human being. As a path of inner awakening, as a path of deep self-knowledge (that is to say, *gnosis*), it invites and supports the inner struggle to attend, to "hear and obey" one's own Self, God in oneself. As Jean-Yves Leloup suggests, this is the intimate meaning of *Anthropos*: to be *fully human oneself*, the incarnation of God. This is an unknown teaching—not in the philosophical or theological sense, nor in the sense that it has never been said before, but in the sense that our ordinary thoughts and feelings can never really penetrate it. And it is unknown in the sense that we live our lives on the surface of ourselves, not knowing the one thing about our own being that it is necessary for us to know and that would bring us every good we could seriously wish for.

We are speaking of an unknown part of ourselves, which is at the same time the essential part of ourselves: the Teacher within, our genuine identity. The *way*—and it is surely the way that is offered by all the spiritual traditions of the world—is the practice, and the community supporting the practice, that opens a relationship between our everyday sense of self and the Self, or *Spirit*. This interior relationship between self and Spirit, we are told, is made possible through the inner cultivation of a specific quality of conscious attention and intelligence that in this tradition is referred to by the Greek term *nous,* or higher mind. It is the realm of intermediate attention and of mediating conscious forces in the cosmos that are mythologized as the angelic realms in the esoteric traditions of the world's religions. It is in this miraculous yet lawful mediating contact between the higher and the lower within ourselves that the deeper, intimate experience of conscious love is given—a conscious love for our starved and confused self that is at the same time love for our neighbor whose inner condition of metaphysical poverty is identical to our own. As Jean-Yves Leloup shows us, this is the love that is spoken of in the words of Jesus, "Thou shalt love thy neighbor as thyself." It is a love that cannot be commanded, but that we are obliged to recognize as the defining attribute of our essential Self.

One of the most remarkable aspects of *The Gospel of Mary Magdalene* is that the more it shows us about the meaning of Christianity, the more the mystery deepens. This paradox is due, surely, to the fact that, like every truly spiritual communication, it speaks to us both on the surface and at deep unconscious levels at the same time. While at the intellectual level it points to the resolution of apparent contradictions that sometimes drive us away from belief in the objective existence of the Good, it at the same time opens the heart to a silent recognition of homecoming—the joy of what we knew without words all along, but had all but given up hope of finding. No mystery is greater or more welcome than this—that above our minds, in the depths of silence, we may be given to know ourselves as Being and as created to serve the good both for God and our neighbor.

Jacob Needleman,
Department of Philosophy,
San Francisco State University,
and author of *Lost Christianity* and *The American Soul*

PREFACE: WHO IS MARY MAGDALENE?

RESEARCH FOR OUR play, *My Magdalene*—about a young woman who finds a challenging and strengthening relationship to Mary Magdalene through her dream life—led us to France, where the Magdalene tradition lives strongly. Halfway up the hill to the cathedral at Vezelay, a nexus of Magdalene devotion, in a little stone bookstore opening onto the steep stone street, Joseph Rowe handed us *The Gospel of Mary Magdalene* in its original French. Completely enchanted by it, we arranged for Mr. Rowe, a very talented translator, dramatist, and musician, to translate it into English.

It became our charge to provide the foreword for this new translation. The fruits of our research, we hoped, would place Mary in some context, thereby, perhaps, making the reading of her gospel more potent.

Accomplishing this meant that we needed to find Mary both historically and geographically. We explored references to her in the Christian Gospels and the Gnostic texts. We traveled to Israel and to the south of France to follow her historical and mythical trail. We reviewed great art of the ages to see how others perceived her. We read as many books as we could find.[1] We asked each other many questions, exploring our own perceptions. And we meditated and prayed for guidance and insight. Our search is not over. It continues to be a remarkable journey.

We consider her reemergence and a renewed awareness of her importance as an essential remembering of the Feminine. The way in which Jean-Yves Leloup honors Mary Magdalene's presence in his commentaries on her gospel contributes greatly to the convergence of her memory with the priceless wisdom of "direct knowing" (the true meaning of *gnosis*).

The earliest materials that refer to Mary Magdalene appear from two very different sources: the canonical Gospels of the New Testament, and a group of fringe materials that have come to be known as the Gnostic

[1]Selected bibliography: Susan Haskins, *Mary Magdalene: Myth and Metaphor* (New York: Riverhead Books, 1993); and Antti Marjanen, *The Woman Jesus Loved: Mary Magdalene in the Nag Hammadi Library & Related Documents* (Leiden: E. J. Brill, 1996), give the best overview of the material. Margaret Starbird has written a very accessible and briefer book, *The Woman with the Alabaster Jar: Mary Magdalen and the Holy Grail* (Santa Fe: Bear, 1993). Laurence Gardner, *Bloodline of the Holy Grail* (Rockport, Mass.: Element, 1996), picks up on earlier work in Michael Baigent, Richard Leigh, and Henry Lincoln, *Holy Blood, Holy Grail* (New York: Little, Brown & Co., 1983). Ean Begg, *The Cult of the Black Virgin*, rev. (New York: Penguin/Arkana, 1996), contains a wealth of new material on the feminine lineage. Lynn Picknett and Clive Prince, *The Templar Revelation: Secret Guardians of the True Identity of Christ* (New York: Touchstone, 1997), spins a fascinating tale at the outer reaches of current thought. All of these books are extremely well researched. If you don't agree with their conclusions, you cannot ignore the meticulous research which they have accomplished.

Another set of works reveal the details of Jesus Christ's life in more complete detail. These include Robert Powell, *Chronicle of the Living Christ: The Life and Ministry of Jesus Christ: Foundations for a Cosmic Christianity* (Hudson, N.Y.: Anthroposophic Press, 1996), which extends the wonderful work of the clairvoyant German nun, Anne Catherine Emmerich, who died in 1826 at age 20, from the four-volume set, *The Life of Jesus Christ and Biblical Revelations* (Rockford, Ill.: Tan Books, 1914 and 1979). The recent book by Neil Douglas-Klotz, *The Hidden Gospel of Jesus Christ* (Wheaton, Ill.: Quest, 1999), brings the most modern of Biblical scholarship into a fresh understanding of the words of Jesus and their fuller meaning.

The Gnostic texts can be found in James Robinson, ed., *The Nag Hammadi Library*, rev. ed. (San Francisco: Harper, 1990); Bentley Layton, *The Gnostic Scriptures* (New York: Doubleday, 1987); G. R. S. Mead, trans., *Pistis Sophia* (Blauvelt, N.Y.: Spiritual Science Library, 1984); and any of the recent books on the Dead Sea Scrolls. Commentaries on these texts in terms of the feminine can be found in Karen King, *Images of the Feminine in Gnosticism* (Harrisburg, Va.: Trinity Press Intl., 1988).

Further, we have made a videotape about this research entitled *Rediscovering Mary Magdalene*, which is available from www.TheStarHouse.org.

gospels, which were rejected by the Roman Catholic Church.

The story of the suppression of these alternative gospels reads like an adventure novel—book burnings, secret meetings of small sects found out by the authorities, exiles, executions, and so forth.

Ironically, the greatest suppression of early Christian literature began when Constantine became emperor of Rome and declared Christianity the religion of the entire Roman Empire (leading to a process of conversion that occurred over a number of years, from his initial victory in 312 C.E. to the final defeat of his rivals in 324). In 325, Constantine convened the Council of Nicaea where it was decided which texts would become the standards of the Church—those that we now know as the canonical Gospels—and which would be suppressed. Those not chosen as standard were attacked—sometimes violently—for many years. Indeed, the bishops at the Council of Nicaea who disagreed with Constantine's choices were exiled on the spot.[2]

The suppression, however, was not completely successful. Some texts survived, passed on since ancient times. Many scraps and fragments turned up in a variety of places over the years, though hardly a significant number. But in 1945 the story took a completely different turn when a stash of alternative texts was found in a large clay jar in the desert at Nag Hammadi, near Phou, Egypt. The account of how these documents traveled from the nomadic tribesmen who discovered them, through the black markets—one of the papyrus books from the jar even found its way into the possession of the Swiss psychologist Carl Jung—and eventually back to Cairo makes a true adventure tale.[3] The contents of this jar, along with other scraps or fragments from around the same time period, have become known as the Gnostic gospels, because of the association of many of them with the belief system of a group who called themselves Gnostics, from the Greek word *gnosis*, meaning "inner knowing," "self-acquaintance," or

---

[2] James Carroll, *Constantine's Sword* (New York: Houghton Mifflin, 2001).

[3] Stephan Hoeller gives the best telling of the story of the discovery of these documents in *Jung and the Lost Gospels* (Wheaton, Ill.: Theosophical Publishing House, 1989).

"self-knowledge." Amidst the often very strange cosmology of the Gnostic sects, there can be found what has come to be known as *gnosticism,* the belief that spiritual development and salvation are achieved through inner knowing. Recent writers have seized on the modern aspects of these texts, finding in them leading-edge thinking about intuition and consciousness. In reality, while the Gospel of Thomas (one of those discovered at Nag Hammadi) and the Gospel of Mary Magdalene are often considered Gnostic texts, and while they do share the same emphasis on inner knowing, they do not share the elaborate cosmology of the treatises from the Gnostic sects.[4]

The discovery of the Nag Hammadi texts gave a much fuller picture of the body of materials rejected early in the history of Christianity and sparked interest in studying other incomplete texts that had been languishing in the vaults of museums. One of these texts receiving renewed interest was the Gospel of Mary, found in Egypt in 1896 and left to the care of the Berlin Museum. The rediscovery of this gospel resulted in a number of translations—the first in 1955—and this translation from the Coptic to French by Jean-Yves Leloup, a scholar who has a deep intellectual and spiritual understanding of the whole range of early scriptures, and who has commented on many of them.

Besides translating the texts found in Egypt, scholars have attempted to determine their ages. Most scholars believe that the jar discovered at Nag Hammadi was placed there around 350 C.E. and that the Coptic texts in it were translations from Greek originals. How old, then, were the original writings? Complex textual analysis can lead only to educated guesses. Some scholars believe that the text of the Sayings of Jesus in the Gospel of Thomas goes back to 50 C.E., that it predates the canonical Gospels, and that it may be contemporaneous with the "Q" text thought to be the common (missing) sourcebook for the canonical Gospels. Some

---

[4]The Gospel of Mary was not found in the jar unearthed at Nag Hammadi. It had been found earlier in Egypt, in 1896, and resides now in Berlin. This document was, however, included in Robinson's *The Nag Hammadi Library* because it and the three other tracts that were found in 1896 are completed by—as they complement—the much larger find at Nag Hammadi.

think that other portions of the Gnostic gospels date to no earlier than the third century, while others suggest that the Gospel of Mary Magdalene may date to the early part of the second century.[5]

Ultimately, all that we know is not enough to allow us to determine the exact historical origins of the Gospel of Mary in either time or place. Once we have exhausted historical certainties, however, we can determine something of the context of this work and its author through other means.

᷁

We have four ways to explore a life story that goes as far back in time as that of Mary Magdalene. First, we can review the available references to her in the canonical Gospels and the Gnostic texts. Some of the Gnostic texts feature Magdalene prominently and convey a very different picture from the Gospels we're familiar with, including the presentation of Magdalene as the intimate companion of Jesus, while the references presented in the canonical Gospels themselves can be examined for their deeper resonance.

Second, we can approach the story through the eyes and experiences of the great artists who have focused on scenes from the Gospel references to Mary and have interpreted them through their own intuitions (filtered, of course, through the views of their cultural context). In reviewing art from books and tramping through museums around the world, we have been fascinated by several recurring symbolic interpretations: Magdalene is often painted with red or golden hair; she is repeatedly associated with a jar used for anointing; and many times she is depicted in the presence of a skull.

A third way to approach the story of the Gospel of Mary and the significance of Mary herself is to explore both on a purely symbolic level, much as artists have done with their recurring images. Doing so enables us to pose and, perhaps answer, the questions: What does this woman

---

[5]Marjanen, *The Woman Jesus Loved: Mary Magdalene in the Nag Hammadi Library & Related Documents,* and Haskins, *Mary Magdalene: Myth and Metaphor,* summarize the work of many authors, including the Jesus Seminar and the researchers on the lost "Q" gospel. Marjanen dates the Gospel of Mary to the middle of the second century (*The Woman Jesus Loved,* 97–98).

represent to us today, and what is the symbolic significance of her words and actions?

Last, an approach to Mary and her existence can be a particularly spiritual exploration. What has fueled our personal research is that we perceive a profound and important spiritual truth embodied by Mary Magdalene and her unique relationship with Jesus, one that has been ignored or edited from the last two millennia.

ॐ

The canonical Gospels (Matthew, Mark, Luke, and John) mention Mary Magdalene by name a handful of times, though many have assigned to her the identity of other unnamed women who figure in these four texts. For instance, there has been some assumption that she and Mary of Bethany, Lazarus's sister, are the same person. Likewise, Luke refers to a woman, a "sinner"—often assumed to be a prostitute—who brings unguent to anoint Jesus at the home of Simon, a Pharisee, and some have believed that Magdalene is this sinner who receives forgiveness after washing Jesus' feet with her tears (Luke 7:36–50).

Mary's identity as a prostitute stems from *Homily 33* of Pope Gregory I, delivered in the year 591, in which he declared that she and the unnamed woman in Luke 7 are, in fact, one and the same, and that the faithful should hold Mary as the penitent whore:

> She whom Luke calls the sinful woman, whom John calls Mary, we believe to be the Mary from whom seven devils were ejected according to Mark. And what did these seven devils signify, if not all the vices? . . . It is clear, brothers, that the woman previously used the unguent to perfume her flesh in forbidden acts.[6]

It is interesting to note that the Greek word interpreted as "sinner" in the verse of Luke to which Pope Gregory referred was *harmartolos*, which can

---

[6]Haskins, *Mary Magdalene: Myth and Metaphor*, 93.

be translated several ways. From a Jewish perspective, it could mean one who has transgressed Jewish law. It might also mean someone who, perhaps, did not pay his or her taxes. The word itself does not imply a streetwalker or a prostitute. The Greek word for harlot, *porin,* which is used elsewhere in Luke, is not the word used for the sinful woman who weeps at Jesus' feet. In fact, *there is no direct reference to her—or to Mary—as a prostitute anywhere in the Gospels.*

Amidst all of the conjecture regarding the identity of Mary we find some important details that do emerge from all four Gospels: Mary Magdalene is the only woman besides Mother Mary who is mentioned by name in all four texts, and her name, in all but one instance, is the first listed when there is mention of the women present at an event. The texts also clearly indicate that Jesus heals Mary Magdalene by freeing her from seven demons (Mark 16:9, Luke 8:2), an event referred to by Pope Gregory in *Homily 33.* We learn, as well, that she is one of the three, along with John the Apostle and Mother Mary, who waits at the foot of the cross during Christ's crucifixion (John 19:25). And, most essentially, we know that Mary Magdalene is the first to see Jesus Christ resurrected from the tomb (John 20:11–18, Mark 16:9, Matthew 28:9–10). It is because of this that she is considered the "apostle of apostles," and is so called even by Saint Augustine.

Altogether, these few specifics seems so paltry, so scant! Yet they give us enough to work with, if we can understand their condensed meanings. Each of these references translates something more than its face value and provides more insight about Mary.

We hear in the Gospels about many healings—of the crowds of sick and needy gathering to receive Jesus' touch or glance.[7] But only in the case of Mary Magdalene are seven demons released from one person. The usual

---

[7]Anne Catherine Emmerich's four volumes of writings, *The Life of Jesus Christ and Biblical Revelations,* fill out the picture of the healings through the years of Jesus' ministry.

conclusion has been that this exceptional number of demons must stem directly from the depth of her sin. But there may be another interpretation, which lies in the number seven.

Since ancient times, spiritual science has understood that human beings have seven energy centers located throughout the body. These "wheels of energy" are called *chakras* in Sanskrit. The understanding of chakras can be traced from the earliest teachings in India, to the cultures of Babylon and Assyria, then to the culture of Egypt. From there, it entered the traditions of the Hebrews—there are many references to the sevenfold structure of spiritual worlds in Hebrew scripture and thought that the Hebrews themselves claimed to have received as divine revelation, but which also may have been absorbed during their captivities in Babylon and Egypt.[8]

The Hebrew menorah reflects this numerical and spiritual connection: the six candles reach up to the seventh, central light of the spirit. Today the awareness of the body's seven energy centers is the focus of the spiritual science of many healers who work with chakras and the seven levels.[9]

Unfortunately, the fact that Mary Magdalene is freed from the possession of seven demons has resulted in greater focus on the perceived stigma of her past as interpreted in *Homily 33* than on her cleansed state after this healing. Only in 1969 did the Catholic Church officially repeal Gregory's labeling of Mary as a whore, thereby admitting their error—though the image of Mary Magdalene as the penitent whore has remained in the public teachings of all Christian denominations. Like a small erratum buried in

---

[8]There are over three hundred uses of the word *seven* in the Hebrew Bible and New Testament. Many of them speak about time or a number of offspring. Some speak in ways that can only be understood symbolically, such as the seven pillars of wisdom (Proverbs 9), the seven cleansings in the river Jordan (2 Kings 5), the seven circuits of the trumpets around the city of Jericho (Joshua 6), the seven eyes of God in the stone (an amazing picture of the chakras in the human body, in Zechariah 3 and 4), and the many references in Daniel. The tradition of Kabbalah interprets all of these, including the references to time, as veiled references to deep secrets about human and divine energy.

[9]Barbara Brennan, a highly trained scientist who worked for NASA, has systematized the chakra system in her practical method of healing, *Hands of Light* (New York: Pleiades, 1987).

the back pages of a newspaper, the Church's correction goes unnoticed, while the initial and incorrect article continues to influence readers.

But it's important to remember that Jesus Christ does relieve Mary of the seven demons—or, perhaps, those aspects that can cloud vision and energy at each of the seven chakras. Presumably, she no longer possesses the seven deadly sins—pride, lust, envy, anger, covetousness, gluttony, and sloth. In their place exist the corresponding virtues[10]—the way has been cleared for "the seven virgins of light." [11] If her purification is viewed in this way, it makes her the most thoroughly sanctified person mentioned in the New Testament. Imagine being completely cleansed of prejudice and old grudges, fogs of illusion, hereditary obstacles to health, all desires. Once healed, she can truly see the spiritual truth that works in all things. She can see the barbarity of other human beings, as well as the transcendent beauty of Jesus Christ's teachings. In modern terms, her heart and energetic centers are open.

On the third morning after the Crucifixion, Mary Magdalene feels a call to visit Jesus' tomb. She takes with her a container of unguent, perhaps one in the series of ancient oils used to assist the dead through the underworld and into the realms of spirit. She alone meets Jesus Christ at the tomb in his resurrected body. It is easy to imagine that she receives an important teaching here, one that can be comprehended only by a person whose seven demons have been lifted.

The evangelists John, Mark, and Matthew all relate this first appearance to Mary of the risen Christ. The brief verbal exchange that then

---

[10]The Rosicrucians imagined that pride found its elevation in humility, lust in brotherly/sisterly love, envy in love for knowledge, anger in self-controlled directed will, covetousness in poverty or independence, gluttony in both steadfastness and silence in the inner search, and sloth in love for all of life. Thus Magdalene had all the seven virtues plus the important virtue of having known the seven vices, an experience that leads to compassion for others.

[11]*Pistis Sophia*, 271, a most beautiful image of cleansed and renewed energy centers. The *Pistis Sophia* has been criticized as a highly edited third-century (at the earliest) version of an earlier *Questions of Mary*, unfortunately lost. We can find in its writings, however, wonderful hints about Mary's reputation.

occurs between Christ and Mary as related in the Gospel of John has spurred much debate. When she understands that the man she has assumed is the gardener is actually her teacher, she speaks the intimate word *rabboni,* and reaches toward him. Jesus Christ responds, in the King James version (John 20:17), "Do not touch me." The Latin translation is, *"Noli me tangere."* These words have been interpreted as confirmation that Mary Magdalene still carries some of the taint from her sins. In other words, some perceive Jesus Christ's words as, "Stay away from me, you soiled woman." Indeed, many statues with the inscription, *Noli me tangere* depict a transcendent Jesus Christ and a woman below him, groveling in the ultimate shame of rejection.

Were Mary Magdalene still soiled from her past, however, then we would have to conclude that Jesus Christ is not really an effective healer— that he hadn't really done the job of cleansing her of her demons. If we look at Christ's words in the original Greek, the meaning translates a little differently. *"Me mou aptou"* uses the imperative mood of the verb *(h)aptein,* "to fasten." A better translation would then be, "Don't hold onto me" or "Don't cling to me."

Now for the full line: "Do not cling to me, for I am not yet ascended to the Father." The last part of the sentence takes on the greater importance—Jesus Christ refers to the nature of the resurrected body that exists between the earthly body and the ascended body, a nature which we could think of as the *eidolon,* that is, the "pure and ideal image." [12]

When we let go of the emphasis on Mary Magdalene's rejection that some hear in Jesus' words outside the tomb, and see this instead as a teaching about the other worlds in which we can exist, we can then understand that these words may indicate her very special role. She is the one—perhaps, because of her purified state, the only one—who can deliver Christ's message: "Go to my brethren and tell them I ascend to my Father and your Father, and my God and your God." At this point, she

---

[12]The resurrection body as a "pure and ideal image" is explained best of all by Rudolf Steiner in *The Fifth Gospel* (New York: Anthroposophic Press, 1974).

becomes in the canonical Gospels the "apostle of apostles," which the other gospels (from Nag Hammadi, the third-century *Pistis Sophia*, and so forth) expand upon.[13] Jesus clearly asks her to represent a teaching to the others—to the men who were not to be found at the foot of the cross during the Crucifixion, the men who did not believe Jesus himself when he told them he would rise.

Do we know what she taught? The Gospel of Mary Magdalene is the primary source of the teaching that she received. Jean-Yves Leloup's commentaries add much insight to the text, which is missing some critical pages, and restores this text to a place of importance which other Gnostic compilations have ignored. In a way, this teaching received by Mary at the site of the Resurrection is the most important one of all.

Tradition hands us a picture of the final moments of Jesus Christ's life on the cross. Three figures stand at his feet, three central people through whom his teachings will go out into the world (John 19:25): Mother Mary, John the Apostle, and Mary Magdalene.

Mother Mary will become the center of the disciples and will focus the descending power of spiritual fire at Pentecost, whereupon the disciples, "filled with the spirit," will go out and preach the gospel, evangelize, convert, and baptize. The so-called apostolic succession means that official Christianity has come through the successive initiations of priest to priest, beginning with Peter. Mother Mary, as the human progenitor at the beginning of this line of succession, becomes the mysterious figure onto whom the faithful project all hidden needs. The tradition of succession, this spiritual stream beginning with the virgin birth of Jesus, concentrates on the outer work of the Church, on telling the Good News of the Gospels, on proselytizing to convince and convert others to this understanding.

---

[13]For example, from the *Pistis Sophia*, 193: "Where I shall be, there will be also my twelve ministers. But Mary Magdalene, John, and the Virgin will tower over all my disciples and over all men who shall receive the mysteries in the Ineffable. And they will be on my right and on my left. And I am they, and they are I."

The second figure, John, will accompany Mother Mary to Ephesus for her final years, become the bishop of Ephesus, and eventually suffer exile to the island of Patmos, where he will receive and record a powerful revelation along with his version of the Gospel story. One can gather all the Johns, including John the Baptist, into John the Apostle's mystical teachings and the way of mysticism that has grown from them.[14]

෧ఫ

But can we identify what lives today from Mary Magdalene's connection to Jesus Christ and her presence at the cross? We see the apostles taking the work of Jesus into the world—but Magdalene was not present at Pentecost. Based on our studies of Mary Magdalene, we imagine the idea of proselytizing did not resonate with her direct experience of the Divine. Perhaps her kind of wisdom was not something she could preach about. Instead, Mary Magdalene focuses on the inner worlds of initiation.

We imagine that, not through outer pomp and pageantry, but through gnosis or direct knowing, she seeks union with the Divine. Hers is the path of the sacred marriage,[15] accomplished within.

Her path emphasizes inner preparation, introspection, and inner transformation. Perhaps, in addition, she also represents the feeling world; she carries the sensitivity of sensuality, in the truest meaning of the word, finding the divinity in the senses.

In addition, the presence of Mary at the Crucifixion and at the tomb, beyond illustrating her love for Jesus, also indicates her comfort and familiarity with death. The many artistic depictions of Magdalene with a skull may suggest that this has long been seen as part of her identity. In fact, Golgotha, the hill where Jesus was crucified, means "place of the skull." Perhaps visionary artists of the past, in their representations, were implying that Magdalene understands the thresholds of death. Her appearances with

---

[14]Rudolf Steiner and Robert Powell make these links most persuasively.

[15]A favorite theme of Solomon's *Song of Songs*, as well as a theme that is emerging today in many places.

special oils to use in anointing Jesus Christ place her in the tradition of priests and priestesses of Isis, whose unguents were used to achieve the transition over the threshold of death while retaining consciousness.

Jesus accepts and encourages this anointing, explaining to the other disciples that she "helps prepare me for my burial." This statement implies Jesus' knowledge that Mary is aware of what is happening at a deeper level than the other disciples. We can ask ourselves, "By what authority does she anoint him?" But we cannot ignore the fact that the very word *christ* means "anointed one." How can it be that Christians have pushed into a dark corner the female minister of the rite of anointing?

After one anointing of Christ by Mary, in Mark 14: 9, Jesus remarks, "Verily I say unto you, wheresoever this gospel shall be preached throughout the whole world, what she has done here will be told in remembrance of her." How is it, then, that all Christians do not remember and revere this memorial, so clearly marked by their teacher? Why do most people know her as the reformed prostitute, rather than as what seems more likely—a ministering priestess with a deep understanding of the thresholds of the spirit world?

In the legends and stories told about Mary Magdalene there can be found some hint of what she may represent to us today: As one who was cleansed from sin; who remains with Christ throughout his death on the cross; and who first witnesses, understands, and believes Christ's resurrection, she represents a human being who is open and available to true "inner knowing," who can "see" in deeper, clearer ways through a unique spiritual connection to both earthly death and the Divine. In southern France there is a strong belief that Mary Magdalene journeyed there along with a small band of followers of Jesus Christ after the chaos that prevailed in Jerusalem.

It is said that she lived in the caves that extend throughout the area and developed a kind of *clairvoyance*—"clear seeing"—that permitted her to become intimate with the caverns and passageways without the use of torches. These caves, carved from the region's limestone, extend for hundreds of miles, and make up the most extensive subterranean system in the world. There is one cavern at Ste. Baume, in the hills east of Marseilles, where Mary is said to have lived the last thirty years of her life in intimate connection with this hidden part of the earth.

Each morning, according to another legend, a group of angels lifted Mary Magdalene above the summit of the cliffs where she could listen to the entire choir of angelic hosts, the divine sounds of original and continuing creation.

David Tresemer, Ph.D., and Laura-Lea Cannon

THE GOSPEL
OF MARY MAGDALENE

LIST OF ABBREVIATIONS

NT	New Testament
OT	Old Testament
1 Cor	First Corinthians (NT)
1 Jn	First Letter of John (NT)
1 Sm	I Samuel (OT)
1 Thes	First Thessalonians (NT)
2 Jn	Second Letter of John (NT)
Acts	Acts of the Apostles (NT)
Col	Colossians (NT)
Dt	Deuteronomy (OT)
Eph	Ephesians (NT)
Ex	Exodus (OT)
Gal	Galatians (NT)
Is	Isaiah (OT)
Jn	The Gospel of John (NT)
Jgs	Judges (OT)
Lk	The Gospel of Luke (NT)
Mk	The Gospel of Mark (NT)
Mt	The Gospel of Matthew (NT)
Nm	Numbers (OT)
Prv	Proverbs (OT)
Phil	Philippians (NT)
Rv	Revelation (NT)
Rom	Romans (NT)
Wisdom	Wisdom of Solomon (OT Apocrypha)

INTRODUCTION

ALTHOUGH HISTORIANS of early Christianity now have many gospels in their catalogues, those of Matthew, Mark, Luke, and John remain the best known. For most churches, they are still the only ones authorized to communicate to us the echoes and interpretations of the events and teachings that took place in Galilee and Judaea about twenty centuries ago.

The recent discovery in 1945 of the library of Nag Hammadi in Upper Egypt has enabled us to broaden our horizons and enrich our knowledge of certain aspects of Christianity that had previously been hidden or suppressed by the orthodoxies. The gospels contained in this library are written in the Sahidic Coptic language (the word *copt* comes from the Arabic *qibt*, which in turn is a contraction of the Greek *Aiguptos,* or Egypt). Most of them are attributed to direct disciples of the Galilean rabbi Yeshua, considered by some to be the Messiah foretold by Hebraic scriptures, by others as a prophet or a teacher—and by still others as the universal Savior.

Today we are able to study these other gospels—of Philip, Peter, Bartholomew, and most especially of Thomas—right alongside those of Matthew, Mark, Luke, and John. As with some other gospels that came later, it has been established that the Gospel of Thomas (Thomas being also the name of the evangelist of India whose tomb is believed to be in Madras) contains certain *logia*, or simple sayings, that are likely to be older than the revisions of the canonical texts, and may have been skillfully used by the editors of the latter.[1]

Among these other gospels, which have recently become much better known, there is one that does not seem to have attracted the attention it deserves from specialists and is still practically unknown to the public at large. It is the Gospel of Mary, attributed to Miriam of Magdala (Mary Magdalene). Because she was the first witness of the Resurrection, she was considered by the apostle John as the founder of Christianity,[2] long before Paul and his vision on the road to Damascus.

By all apostolic accounts, Yeshua of Nazareth himself was certainly not a founder of any "ism," nor of any institution. He was the Annunciator, the Witness, and some would go so far as to say the Incarnation of

---

[1]See Introduction, Translation, and Commentary in Jean-Yves Leloup, *L'Evangile de Thomas* (Paris: Albin Michel,1986).

[Several of the English versions available are included in: James M. Robinson, ed., *The Nag Hammadi Library*, rev. ed. (San Francisco: HarperSan Francisco, 1990); Kloppenborg, ed., Marvin Meyer, trans., *The Q-Thomas Reader* (Polebridge Press, 1994), a bilingual Coptic/English edition with rich notes and commentary; and Funk, Hoover, and the Jesus Seminar, *The Five Gospels* (New York: Scribner, 1993). Each of the latter two books includes a textual comparison of the Gospel of Thomas with each of the four canonical Gospels, as well as with the lost, hypothetical "Q" source of the sayings of Jesus.

It is not certain that the Thomas who preached in India and the author of the Gospel of Thomas are the same person. Today's so-called Thomas Christians of India reject this scripture and have long been allied with the Church of Rome.

To complicate things further, there are a number of other scriptures attributed to this apostle that are definitely not from the same source, nor of the same quality, as the Gospel of Thomas. This has led to a surprising amount of confusion. For example, even A. N. Wilson, author of the bestselling book *Jesus* (New York: Harper Collins Flamingo, 1993, 82–84), completely mistakes the Gospel of Thomas for the very different *Infancy Gospel of Thomas*, an unrelated writing of vastly lower quality.—*Trans.*]

[2]See Jn 20. All translations agree on this point.

the possible reign of the Spirit in the heart of this space-time, the manifestation of the Infinite in the very heart of our finitude, the voice of the
Other within the speech of human beingness.

The Gospel of Mary makes up the first part of the so-called Berlin
Papyrus.[3] This manuscript was acquired in Cairo by C. Reinhardt and has
been preserved since 1896 in the Egyptology section of the National
Museum of Berlin. It probably came from the area of Akhmin, since it
first appeared in an antique shop in that town. According to C. Schmidt,
this copy was made in the early fifth century. The papyrological analysis
of the manuscript was done by W. C. Till, following the work of C.
Schmidt, and then corrected and completed by H. M. Schenke[4] The
scribe wrote down twenty-one, twenty-two, or twenty-three lines per
page, with each line containing an average of twenty-two or twenty-three
letters. Several leaves are missing[5] from the document: pages 1 to 6, and
11 to 14. This renders its interpretation particularly difficult.

Like the other writings in the Berlin Papyrus, and also like the
Gospel of Thomas, the Gospel of Mary is written in Sahidic Coptic, with
a number of dialectical borrowings. Several faulty transcriptions and other
errors have been discerned in the writing.

As to the dating of the original text upon which the copy was based, it is
interesting to note that there exists a Greek fragment—the Rylands Papyrus
463—whose identity as the precursor of the Coptic text has been confirmed
by Professor Carl Schmidt. This fragment comes from Oxyrhynchus and

---

[3]See W. Beltz, *Katalog der koptishen Handschriften*, 97.

[Curiously, no translation of the Gospel of Mary was made available to the public at large until
some years after the independent discoveries at Nag Hammadi and Qumran—*Trans.*]

[4]See W. C. Till, *Die gnostischen Schriften des koptischen Papyrus Berolinensis 8502 (Tu 60)* (Berlin,
1955); 2d edition: H. M. Schenke (Berlin, 1972); H. M. Schenke, *Bemerkungen zum koptischen
Papyrus Berolinensis 8502*, 315–22.

[5]The average size of the leaves is 13.5 cm. x 10.5 cm. The pages are numbered at the top.

dates from the beginning of the third century.[6] The first edition of the Gospel of Mary, however, would likely be older than this, that is, from sometime during the second century. W. C. Till places it around the year 150. Therefore it would seem, like the canonical Gospels, to be one of the founding or primitive texts of Christianity. If this is so, what is the reason for the general reticence about reading and discussing it?

Today's reactions are essentially the same as those of Peter and Andrew themselves, after they had listened to Miriam of Magdala:

> *Then Andrew began to speak, and said to his brothers:*
> *"Tell me, what do you think of these things she has been*
>   *telling us?*
> *As for me, I do not believe*
> *that the Teacher would speak like this.*
> *These ideas are too different from those we have known."*
> *And Peter added:*
> *"How is it possible that the Teacher talked*
> *in this manner, with a woman,*
> *about secrets of which we ourselves are ignorant?*
> *Must we change our customs,*
> *and listen to this woman?*
> *Did he really choose her, and prefer her to us?"*
>
>   (Mary 17:9–20)

The difficulty of acceptance of this text turns out to be one of the most interesting things about it.

For this is a gospel that was at least inspired (if not literally written down) by a woman: Miriam of Magdala. Here she is neither the sinful

---

[6]See C. H. Roberts, *Catalogue of the Greek and Latin Papyrus*, p. 20. Bibliography and translation in A. de Santos, *Los Evangelios apocrifos*, 100–01.

[According to the Jesus Seminar (see note 1 above, *The Five Gospels*, 128), the Gospel of Mary was written even earlier in the second century, during the same period as the last redactions of the Gospel of John. This would support the author's thesis that it influenced early Christian writings in spite of the fact that it was later suppressed by the emergent orthodoxy.—*Trans.*]

woman of the canonical Gospels, nor is she the woman of more recent traditions, which confuse her sin with some sort of misuse of the lively power of her sexuality.

Here, she is the intimate friend of Yeshua, and the initiate who transmits his most subtle teachings.

ᘓᘏ

An even deeper difficulty to acceptance of the Gospel of Mary arises from the nature of its teaching, from the anthropology[7] and the metaphysics that are implicit in it. This is not a dualistic anthropology, nor is it a metaphysics of Being, with the essences to which we have become accustomed in Western philosophy. It is instead a fourfold anthropology, and a metaphysics of the Imaginal, whose keys the most liberated and informed minds of our era have just begun to rediscover.

MIRIAM OF MAGDALA

Among all the gospels attributed to men, we have in the Gospel of Mary a text attributed to a woman—the one whom the other disciples acknowledge as having first seen the resurrected Christ (cf. Mk 16:9; Jn 20:18). In the early centuries of Christian writings, there was scarcely a text to be found that did not mention her, sometimes to glorify her, other times in an attempt to minimize her importance.

In addition to the gospel that is our concern here, two other writings also bear her name: the *Questions of Mary*, mentioned by Epiphanus,[8] and *The Birth of Mary*, one passage of which is also mentioned by him.[9]

Miriam of Magdala assumes her full importance in the *Questions of*

---

[7][It is important to bear in mind that the author uses the word *anthropology* (*anthropologie*, in French) throughout this book in a non-standard way. He means it in its original, pre-modern sense of a comprehensive philosophy of human nature and its place in the cosmos. Thus there are many possible anthropologies.—*Trans.*]

[8]*The Panarion*, XXVI, 8:1 and 2 (French translation), in *Tel Quel*, no. 88, pp. 70–71, 85–86.

[9]*The Panarion*, XXVI, 12:1–4 (French translation), in *Tel Quel*, no. 88, p. 75, 88.

Mary, yet this same document was also used as a model for a very different text by a later author. In that later work, the *Questions of Mary* was rewritten and revised so as to take on a markedly dualistic and ascetic character, and the role of Mary somehow became strangely minimized and devalued.

Although the original *Questions of Mary* has been lost, and is known only through the quotations given by Epiphanus, the dualistic redaction was developed into a long Coptic manuscript, which now resides in the British Library, Additional 5114, known since the eighteenth century under the title of the *Pistis Sophia*.[10]

According to Michel Tardieu, editor of the Berlin Codex, the author or authors of the Gospel of Mary "sought to take a position in the debate over the role of Miriam of Magdala; the canonical Gospels already contain hints of stories about this subject." Tardieu's further reflections on this are worth quoting at length:

> All of these gospels recognize that she had belonged to the group of women who had followed Jesus, that she had been present at his death on the cross, and that she was the first (Mk 16:9) to whom he appeared on the morning of the Resurrection. It is probably due to the latter belief that she was considered as foremost among the women who followed Jesus.
>
> Also, it is said in that same verse of Mark, as well as in Luke 8:3, that Jesus had driven seven demons from her. This is a personality full of contrast—initially possessed by demons, then companion to Jesus and first witness of the Resurrection. There is already plenty here to nourish the Christian imagination. The Mary Magdalene who serves as the poetic foundation of the gospel of Codex B has become at once the confidante of Jesus, his interpreter, and his replacement: Jesus divulges words to her that are unknown to the other disciples; she occupies the place left vacant by him, and she communicates and explains the secrets that she received from him.

---

[10]French translation by E. Amelineau (Arché-Milan, 1975). In English, see also G. R. S. Mead, *The Pistis Sophia: A Gnostic Gospel* (Kessinger, 1997).

This role as intermediary between Jesus and the other disciples is supported by a belief in Mary Magdalene as the companion of Jesus during his lifetime and as the first witness of the Resurrection. It seems only natural that she who has followed Jesus everywhere and is there on Easter morning has been accorded special revelations. In the common belief of Jesus' followers, the post-Resurrection time is one of decisive revelations, which include his communication of the mission given the disciples before his final departure. Because she is the first to have "seen the Lord" (Jn 20:18), her presence among the disciples listening to her report of his last words is an imposing theme, and one that is important for the gospels of the post-Resurrection.

Some later authors were led to elaborate this theme in the form of a sort of erotic-mystical novel: Mary Magdalene is the confidante of Jesus because she is his sexual partner (*Questions of Mary*). This is the origin of the Encratite reaction, which shows up in the exegetical and theological London manuscript *(Pistis Sophia)*, where Mary Magdalene is only one of the protagonists in the general discussion that takes place between Jesus and the disciples.[11]

It is possible that the editor of Codex B (the Berlin Codex), by selecting precisely this gospel to bear the name of Mary, intended to take a stance in this debate and to counter the excesses of the *Questions of Mary*. But the authorship of the gospel is not important to the debate. The woman who is in the spotlight is the Mary Magdalene of the New Testament. The poetic details that are supplied (reports of visions, the jealousy of the disciples, her tears) change nothing of the essential personality whom Syrian-Palestinian Christianity credited as the ultimate confidante of Jesus, and the revealer of the *logia* of the Master.[12]

---

[11][The London manuscript is now referred to as the *Pistis Sophia*. In it the role of Mary is eclipsed.— Trans.]

[12]Long quotation from J. M. Tardieu, *Codex de Berlin* (Editions du Cerf, 1984), 24.

But perhaps we could be more simple and direct than this, and join with the Gospel of John (11:5) in saying that the Lord loved her as he loved her sister Martha, her brother Lazarus, and the other men and women who followed him, including Judas.

Yeshua did not love John or Peter *more* than he loved Judas, but rather he loved each differently. He loved them all with a universal and unconditional love and each of them in a unique and particular fashion. With regard to the unique and particular nature of his relationship with Mary Magdalene, the Gospel of Philip insists, for example, that Mary is the special companion of Jesus (*koinonos*).

Yeshua invites us to experience our capacity for a divine love that includes all beings, even our enemies. But human love includes preferences—in other words, affinities, resonances, and intimacies that are not possible with everyone.

> The Lord loved Mary more than all the disciples, and often used to kiss her on the mouth. When the others saw how he loved Mary, they said "Why do you love her more than you love us?" The Savior answered them in this way: "How can it be that I do not love you as much as I love her?" [13]

Those who are unaware of the founding texts of early Christianity are still shocked by the first sentence of this passage from the Gospel of Philip. It is not my intention to take sides in the polemics around this subject. Some partisans in this debate maintain that Jesus had an obligation to be married because he taught in synagogues; Jewish tradition considers an unmarried man to be either incomplete or disobedient toward God, and he is therefore not allowed to teach in synagogues. Even less could an unmarried man be a priest who is allowed to enter the

---

[13]See the Gospel of Philip 59:9.

holiest parts of the Temple.[14] But others retort that Yeshua also kept company with John the Baptist and the Essenes, and that we know from the so-called Dead Sea Scrolls (not to be confused with the Nag Hammadi texts) found at Qumran that these Essenes were not only unmarried, but rejected "women, sinners, and the weak."[15] If we stick to the familiar gospels, there is no indication that Yeshua was married (at least, not in any formal sense of the word). Nevertheless, it is abundantly clear that he did not reject, but loved and welcomed women, sinners, and the weak. This in itself would have been a scandal not only for Essenes, but also for Pharisees, Sadducees, and Zealots, as well as for other sects of that era.

The real question is not whether Yeshua was married (again, in the formal sense of the word), for why should that be so important? The interesting question is this: Was Yeshua fully human, with a normal human sexuality that was capable of intimacy and preference?

As the ancient proverb says: "That which is not lived is not redeemed." If Yeshua, considered as the Messiah and the Christ (from Greek *christos*, a rendering of the Hebrew *mashiah*), did not live his sexuality, then sexuality would be unredeemed. In that case, he could not be a Savior in the full sense of the word. This eventually led to the institution of a logic in Christianity that was more oriented to death than to life. This was especially the case in Western Roman Christianity:

> Jesus Christ did not live his sexuality;
> therefore sexuality is unredeemed;
> therefore sexuality is essentially a bad thing;
> therefore living your sexuality can be degrading
> and can make you *guilty,*

[14]Simon Ben Schorim, *Mon frère Jésus* (Editions du Seuil); also A. Abecassis and Josy Eisenberg, *À Bible ouverte*, vol. 1 (Paris: Albin Michel, 1978), 125.

[15]See also Josephus, *History of the Jews*, Loeb Classical Library (Cambridge, Mass.: Harvard University Press).

This kind of guilt-ridden sexuality can make us truly ill. Thus the very origin of our life, in its physical sense—"in the image of the Creator"—is logically transformed into an instrument of death. Could it be that we Westerners, driven by our collective unconscious guilt, are still suffering the consequences of this logic today?

The Gospel of Mary, like the Gospels of John and of Philip, reminds us that Yeshua was capable of intimacy with a woman. This intimacy was not merely of the flesh, it was also emotional, intellectual, and spiritual. What is at stake here is total salvation, the liberation of a human being in his or her entirety through the imbuing of all dimensions of this being with consciousness and love. By invoking the realism of Yeshua's humanity in its sexual dimension, the Gospel of Mary in no way detracts from his spiritual and divine nature, the dimension of Pneuma [Holy Spirit—*Ed.*].

Mark and Matthew devote more attention to his tears at the plight of Jerusalem, and even his anguish and doubts when faced with death.[16] This is yet another version of Yeshua's humanity, reflecting the belief that it is through such humanity that God is revealed.

The Gospel of Mary, like the canonical Gospels, invites us to free ourselves from the dualisms that tear us apart and render us "demonic." But rather than denying the body or matter, it is by not allowing ourselves to become identified with (and thus enslaved by) any of these partial aspects of the Real that they become sanctified and transfigured. We learn through our *creative imagination* to bring love to those regions where it is lacking—the blocked and stunted areas of our desire and intelligence— just as Miriam of Magdala did, in following her Beloved.

If we wish to experience in our own lives the meaning of the wedding feast at Cana, we must imagine our mutual ignorance transformed through the unexpected Word into a loving friendship that is sweeter and better tasting than the passion of infatuation. The gray waters of the everyday are changed into the spirituous wine of divine love.

---

[16]Mt. 26:39; Mk 14:32; Lk 22:40-46

We ourselves must live the love-filled, waking dream of the Magdalene, where death is met, passed through, and finally understood within the space of the Resurrection.

"THOSE WHO HAVE EARS, LET THEM HEAR"

Not only was Miriam of Magdala a woman, she was a woman who had access to sacred knowledge. Given the era in which she lived, this is enough to have rendered her an outcast or a sinner in many eyes. She was outside the laws of a society where such knowledge is strictly the affair of men, where women were prohibited from studying the secrets of the Torah, or even from learning to read its script.

In her gospel her way of speaking to the disciples is bound to irritate them—Who does she think she is? As if her special status as Yeshua's beloved is not enough, she goes so far as to appropriate his teaching, acting like some sort of initiate. She even uses the same words he had resorted to when faced with somewhat narrow and unprepared minds that can only recognize reality within the small field of their own perceptions: "Those who have ears, let them hear!"

But while these words amount to an annoyance to the disciples, reminding them of the limits of their understanding, the Gospel of Mary goes much deeper. It is witness to an altogether different mode of understanding that the masculine mind typically overlooks: a domain of prophetic or visionary knowledge that, though certainly not exclusive to women, definitely partakes of the feminine principle, and is sometimes known as the angelic or Eastern dimension of human knowledge.

The Teacher is questioned on this subject by Miriam of Magdala: What is the organ of true vision? With what eyes is she able to behold the Resurrection? The Teacher's answer to this is clear. The Resurrection can be seen neither with the eyes of the flesh, nor with the eyes of the soul *(psyche)*. This vision is no hallucination, nor is it any sort of fantasy linked to sensory, psychic, or mental stimulation. Furthermore, this gospel tells us that the Resurrection is not to be categorized as a purely spiritual (pneumatic) vision either. Rather, it is a vision of the *nous*[17]—a dimension often forgotten in our anthropologies. In the ancient world, the nous was seen as "the finest point of the soul"; or as some might say today, the "angel of the soul."[18] It gives us access to that intermediate realm between the purely sensory and the purely spiritual, which Henry Corbin so eloquently names as the *imaginal*.[19]

Following Corbin further, we could say that in the Gospel of Mary we are freed from the reductionist dilemma of thought versus extension (Descartes), as well as from a cosmology and epistemology limited to either empirical observation or intellectual understanding. Between these two lies a vast intermediate realm of image and representation that is just as ontologically real as the worlds of sense and intellect. But this world requires a faculty of perception that is peculiar to it alone. This faculty has a cognitive function and a noetic value that are just as real and

---

[17][The exact words of Jesus in Mary 10:16 (see text of the Gospel of Mary, here) are: "There where is the nous, lies the treasure."

The notion of Jesus using Greek philosophical language is not as strange as it might appear to some. The familiar stereotype of Jesus as a simple carpenter who preached *only* in Aramaic is a popular notion for which there is no plausible evidence. Quite the contrary. It is already improbable that any literate resident of multicultural, polyglot first-century Galilee would speak only Aramaic; but the notion that a Jewish spiritual teacher of the extraordinary intelligence and erudition of Jesus would be ignorant of Greek, and speak and teach exclusively in Aramaic, is due more to deeply rooted populist images of Jesus than to scholarship.—*Trans.*]

[18][It is important to remember that the author uses the words *soul* and *spirit* in something close to their original senses, which are significantly different from modern usages (see note 7 above on *anthropology*). In antiquity, the Greek word *psyche* (like the Hebrew word *nephesh*) did not have the same elevated status that the word *soul* assumed in later Christianity, nor was it confused with spirit (*pneuma* in Greek, *ruah* in Hebrew) the way it later came to be, and still is in current usage. For the ancients, the soul included aspects of the mortal body, mind, and emotions, as well as something transcending them. It was an *intermediary* reality between the physical and the spiritual. In a further refinement of this intermediation, the nous appears here as that part of spirit that is closest to psyche. The highest part of spirit (pneuma) is equated by the author with the Holy Spirit, and is usually capitalized as Pneuma.

There is also the problem of the ambiguity of the word *esprit* in French: sometimes it means "spirit," other times "mind." We have mostly translated Leloup's *esprit* (nous) as "spirit," but there are contexts when "mind" has seemed more appropriate.—*Trans.*]

[19]Or the *mundus imaginalis*. See Henry Corbin, *The Voyage and the Messenger* (Berkeley: North Atlantic Books, 1998), 117–134.

true as those pertaining to the worlds of sense perception and intellectual intuition. It is none other than the power of the creative imagination—yet we must beware of confusing this faculty with the *imagination* as the word is ordinarily used. As Corbin says, the so-called modern mind has reduced this word to the realm of fantasy, a world of merely subjective beings and things.

When Ernest Renan says that "all of Christianity was born from the imagination of a woman," he is mistaken, for he is using the word *imagination* in its pejorative, modern sense of something illusory. His thought is conditioned by an anthropology that is ignorant of the categories of the creative imagination in which ancient texts, including sacred scriptures, were conceived and written down.

A living deity who wants to communicate thus necessitates an intermediate realm between God and human, between the invisible and the visible, between the world of immaterial spirits and material bodies. It is in this intermediary imaginal realm that Miriam has her meetings with the resurrected Christ. As with the ancient prophets, God activates the necessary visionary, imaginal forms in her, so as to bring her to the Divine. It is only in this sense that Christianity can indeed be said to be born from the imagination of a woman.

> *"Lord, I see you now in this vision."*
> *And the Lord answered:*
> *"You are blessed, for the sight of me does not disturb you."*
> *(Mary 10:12–15)*

Here, we have gone beyond any metaphysical opposition of subject vs. object (there can be no object without a subject who conceives and represents it, and there can be no subject who is not reacting to an object or environment perceived as external or "other"). We are in the presence of a metaphysics of openness—a place of meeting, confrontation, and merging of subject and object known in their interdependence. Reality is neither objective nor subjective; it is an inclusive third state where the two imaginally become one.[20]

This reveals a field that has been little explored by contemporary philosophies, which still oscillate between the metaphysics of Being (Heidegger) and of Otherness (Lévinas). The task of the next century will surely be one of engagement with this philosophy of openness, or the in-between realm. Philosophy will no longer seek its missing links in Greek or Semitic thought, but in this oriented synthesis—heretofore rejected by both sides—which begins to reveal itself in these early Christian texts. A true renewal of thinking about the source of New Testament writings must pass through a regeneration of the creative imagination, as Christian Jambet suggests in the following:

> For the creative imagination is not so named with some metaphorical intent, nor in a spirit of fiction, but in the full sense of the term: The imagination creates, and is universal creation itself. Every reality is imaginal, because it is able to present itself as a reality. To speak of the imaginal world is nothing less than to contemplate a metaphysics of Being[21] where subject and object are born together in the same creative act of transcendental imagination.[22]

Rather than speaking of the creative thought, we must henceforth speak of the creative imagination—those who desire to understand nature and world events must learn to dream before learning to think. The language of sacred scriptures is one of images and symbols that belongs to dreams more than to the concepts of the sciences. Christian Jambet goes on to say that,

---

[20]Cf. The Gospel of Thomas, logion 22. See the author's book-length translation and exegesis, Jean-Yves Leloup, *L'Evangile de Thomas* (Paris: Albin Michel, 1986).

[21]I prefer the term *openness* here.

[22]Christian Jambet, *La Logique des Orientaux* (Editions du Seuil, 1983), 45.

Reality is nature ordered by laws. This is what scientific discourse tells us, and this is the operation of the imagination which creates that discourse.

We can see that the *mundus imaginalis* should be approached with the same method, in the same perspective. It is a mode of interlinking, of constructing a meaning, of interpreting that world. But it is far from being an attempt to "say it all"—on the contrary, what is constantly occurring is a saying of the One, but only on condition that it "cannot be all." For the One is impossible to say. What is revealed is the failure of any reality to satisfy the desire for the One. The *mundus imaginalis* is the place where what is said is never the "All," but the lack of it, the yearning for it. It is precisely here that desire becomes imagination.[23]

To this, I would also add *transfiguration* and *resurrection*.

It is this realization and incarnation of her desire that Miriam of Magdala is trying to share with us. It is the creative imagination that this gospel wants to awaken in us, while not avoiding a confrontation with the reservations and objections of a philosophy of sense and reason, as represented by Peter and Andrew.

The ethical consequences of such a practice of desire and imagination are clear, and cannot fail to shock Yeshua's other disciples. "There is no sin," it tells us. It is we who continually create sin with our sickly imagination, and then invent laws to make it more comfortable. It is our imagination that needs to be healed. We are responsible for the world in which we live, since it is we who create it. Our lack of enlightened imagination encloses that faculty in a death-orientation and imposes limits upon it wherein our feeling and intelligence have become arrested.

These questions will be further explored in the commentary in the second part of this book. Let us note here that in this gospel attributed to Miriam of Magdala, the creative imagination to which she bears witness is the meeting place where the sensible and the supersensible Divine

---

[23]Ibid., 45.

descend together in a single dwelling. The imagination is the sympathetic resonance of the invisible and the visible, of the spiritual and the physical.

The motivation behind Miriam's imagination is obviously more than just her personal desire and love. She loves a being whom she has known in the world of sense perception, and in whom she has seen the manifestation of the divine Beloved. Through the power of the imaginal, she has spiritualized this being in raising it from its sensory form to its incorruptible image.

As with the disciples at Mount Tabor, the confrontation with Yeshua opens her eyes to his essential Reality, to the archetype that informs him. Her creative imagination imbues all this with such a powerful presence that she can never leave it nor lose it; thus she creates the true Beloved, which constantly accompanies her and illumines her. This Reality is not any sort of psychological illusion, compensation, nor sublimation. It is an awakening to this intermediate world, an experience and a knowledge in which the Christ is offered as contemplation, as the archetype of synthesis that the soul of desire seeks to embrace:

> *The divine lover is spirit without body;*
> *The physical lover is body without spirit;*
> *The spiritual lover possesses spirit and body.*[24]

The apparition that manifests itself to Miriam of Magdala (both inwardly and outwardly) is spirit and body. It is this manifestation that makes Miriam an *anthropos*, a whole human being, an incarnation that responds to the Incarnation of the common Logos informing both body and spirit.

---

[24]Ibn Arabi, quoted in Henry Corbin, *La topographie spirituelle de l'Islam iranien* (La Différence, 1990).

THE TRANSLATION

In addition to the task of imagining the theological, philosophical, and ethical import of this text of early Christianity, we must also recall its historical interest, for it contains precious information about the first Christian communities. Their deliberations and conflicts give us a sad foretaste of the exclusion of the feminine that was later to triumph, and thereby offer us a glimpse of the different modes and practices that inspired these first Christians.

Later Christianity was often reduced to a path of ethical action—although it engaged itself in a positive transformation of the world toward greater justice and integrity, it risked forgetting the transfiguration of this world into a dimension of greater meaning. It overlooked the need to introduce a lightness into the world's density, an imagination that would open it to new possibilities and make it more bearable.

The translation of the Gospel of Mary has also to answer to the call of the creative imagination, without which its text might appear as utterly hermetic, and perhaps insignificant. The two previous French translations of this text are difficult to read, and sometimes contradictory.[25] Yet this is no reflection of any lack of skill, patience, or courage on the part of those scholars who worked with it. Their considerable labors have provided important references for this translation, which nevertheless is quite different from theirs. My own approach, which may be described as both rigorous and free, is a further development of my earlier work at the University of Strasbourg on the Gospel of Thomas and the Gospel of Truth (Jung Codex).[26]

In part one the translation is presented opposite the script of the Coptic text.[27] Even though most readers will not be able to understand

---

[25]Anne Pasquier, *L'Evangile de Marie* (Québec: Presses de l'Université de Laval, 1983); Michel Tardieu, *L'Evangile de Marie* (Paris: Editions du Cerf, 1984).

[26]Principally with Jacques Ménard, a member of the team that directed the publication of the Nag Hammadi Coptic Library in cooperation with the University of Laval in Canada and E. J. Brill Editions at Leiden in Holland.

[27]Ibid.

the Coptic, I hope that it will inspire examination, thereby stimulating imagination and intuition that can lead to the discovery of personal interpretations—which, though lacking in authority, would make up for this in a deeper feeling for the text.

My aim is different from that of the archaeologist, or the brilliant decoder of obscure hieroglyphs. I do not seek to provide scholarly libraries with nuggets of obscure meaning hidden in the convolutions of the text. My desire is to offer, to as many readers as possible, some insight into Christian origins, and to come closer to a true understanding of the one known as the Christ, whose words still reverberate in our culture today. If I succeed in this, it is because I am able to see him through the loving and unassuming eyes of the woman who, according to the Gospels of John, Thomas, and Philip, among others, was his intimate friend:

> *There were three who always walked with the Lord.*
> *Mary, his mother; Mary, her sister;*
> *And Miriam of Magdala, who was called his companion;*
> *For Miriam is his sister, his mother, and his companion.*[28]

COPTIC TEXT AND TRANSLATION

The pagination of the Coptic text and translation follows that of the original manuscript. Here, references to passages from the Gospel of Mary

---

[28]From the French translation of J. E. Ménard, *L'Evangile selon Philippe: Introduction, texte, traduction et commentaire* (Strasbourg, 1967).

[The above version is my translation of the French excerpt quoted by Leloup. However, Wesley Isenberg's English translation of this same passage in *The Nag Hammadi Library* differs, with the last sentence reading: "His sister and his mother and his companion were each a Mary." But that reading leaves us with two puzzles: a pair of sisters having the same name, Mary; and Jesus's aunt Mary being strangely referred to as his sister. By making use of the original Hebrew name Miriam, so as to distinguish the Magdalene from the other Marys, the French translation skillfully circumvents this reference, interpreting the final sentence as referring *only* to the Magdalene, and thereby alluding to her multifaceted role in Jesus's life. Yet the persistent oddity of two sisters named Mary also occurs in Jn 19:25. Ménard mentions this in his commentary, and identifies Jesus' maternal aunt as Mary-Salomé, wife of Cleophas. However this may be, there seems to be no real scholarly consensus about the confusion of the Marys in the canonical Gospels, and the Gospel of Philip does little to clear it up. For an English translation of the latter, see Robinson, *The Nag Hammadi Library. —Trans.*]

always begin with the page number, followed by the line number of this translation. The numbers in the margins of the Coptic text itself are for convenience only, and have no literary significance. They correspond roughly, but not always exactly, to the line numbers in the translation.

[Note on the English translation: Although Jean-Yves Leloup's French translation is, of course, the basis for this one, the emphasis in producing this has been on clarity and readability in English. In seeking to achieve this, previous Coptic-to-English translations have been consulted.—*Trans.*][29]

---

[29]See *The Nag Hammadi Library*. See also the following Internet sites for this and many other related online texts in English:

 The Gospel of Mary and other gnostic texts online: www.gnosis.org
 Gnostic Society Virtual Library: home.online.no/~noetic/libe.htm
 Gospel of Thomas homepage: www.epix.net/~miser17/Thomas.html
 Online gnostic texts: members.xoom.com/_XMCM/book_archive/01/indx.html

PART ONE

The Gospel of
Mary Magdalene

[z]

[.].[8 ±   ].. ⲑ[ⲩ]ⲗⲏ ⳓⲉ ⲛⲁ
ⲟⲩϣ[ⳓ]ⲡ ϫⲛ ⲙⲙⲟⲛ ⲡⲉϫⲉ ⲡⲥⲱⲣ ϫⲉ
ⲫⲩⲥⲓⲥ ⲛⲓⲙ ⲡⲗⲁⲥⲙⲁ ⲛⲓⲙ ⲕⲧⲓⲥⲓⲥ
ⲛⲓⲙ ⲉⲩϣⲟⲡ ⳨ⲛ ⲛⲉⲩⲉⲣⲏⲩ {ⲙ}ⲛ̄
5   ⲙⲁⲩ ⲁⲩⲱ ⲟⲛ ⲉⲩⲛⲁⲃⲱⲗ ⲉⲃⲟⲗ ⲉ
ⲧⲟⲩⲛⲟⲩⲛⲉ ⲙ̄ⲙⲓⲛ ⲙⲙⲟⲟⲩ ϫⲉ ⲧⲉ
ⲫⲩⲥⲓⲥ ⲛⲑⲩⲗⲏ ⲉⲥⲃⲱⲗ ⲉⲃⲟⲗ ⲉⲛⲁ
ⲧⲉⲥⲫⲩⲥⲓⲥ ⲟⲩⲁⲁⲥ ⲡⲉⲧⲉ ⲟⲩⲛ ⲙⲁⲁ
ϫⲉ ⲙ̄ⲙⲟϥ ⲉⲥⲱⲧⲙ̄ ⲙⲁⲣⲉϥⲥⲱⲧⲙ̄
10   ⲡⲉϫⲉ ⲡⲉⲧⲣⲟⲥ ⲛⲁϥ ϫⲉ ⳨ⲱⲥ ⲁⲕⲧⲁ
ⲙⲟⲛ ⲉ⳨ⲱⲃ ⲛⲓⲙ ϫⲱ ⲙⲡⲓⲕⲉⲟⲩⲁ
ⲉⲣⲟⲛ ⲟⲩ ⲡⲉ ⲡⲛⲟⲃⲉ ⲙⲡⲕⲟⲥⲙⲟⲥ
ⲡⲉϫⲉ ⲡⲥⲱⲣ ϫⲉ ⲙ̄ⲛ ⲛⲟⲃⲉ ϣⲟⲡ ⲁⲗ
ⲗⲁ ⲛ̄ⲧⲱⲧⲛ̄ ⲡⲉ†ⲣⲉ ⲙ̄ⲡⲛⲟⲃⲉ ⲉⲧⲉ
15   ⲧⲛ̄ⲉⲓⲣⲉ ⲛ̄ⲛⲉ†ⲛⲉ ⲛ̄ⲧⲫⲩⲥⲓⲥ ⲛⲧⲙⲛ̄ⲧ
ⲛⲟⲉⲓⲕ ⲉⲧ<ⲟⲩ>ⲙⲟⲩⲧⲉ ⲉⲣⲟⲥ ϫⲉ ⲡⲛⲟ
ⲃⲉ ⲉⲧⲃⲉ ⲡⲁⲓ̈ ⲁϥⲉⲓ ⲛ̄ⳓⲓ ⲡⲁⲅⲁⲑⲟ̅
⳨ⲛ ⲧⲉⲧⲙ̄ⲙⲏⲧⲉ ϣⲁ ⲛⲁ ⲫⲩⲥⲓⲥ
ⲛⲓⲙ ⲉϥⲛⲁⲕⲁⲑⲓⲥⲧⲁ ⲙⲙⲟⲥ ⲉ⳨ⲟⲩ̣
20   ⲉⲧⲉⲥⲛⲟⲩⲛⲉ ⲉⲧⲓ ⲁϥⲟⲩⲱ⳨ ⲉⲧⲟⲧϥ
ⲡⲉϫⲁϥ ϫⲉ ⲉⲧⲃⲉ ⲡⲁⲓ ⲧⲉⲧⲛ̄ϣⲱ
[ⲛ]ⲉ ⲁⲩⲱ ⲧⲉⲧⲙ̄ⲙⲟⲩ ϫⲉ ⲧ[⁝ ̄]

[Pages 1–6 are missing.]

[Page 7]

1   [...] *"What is matter?*

2   *Will it last forever?"*

3   *The Teacher answered:*

4   *"All that is born, all that is created,*

5   *all the elements of nature*

6   *are interwoven and united with each other.*

7   *All that is composed shall be decomposed;*

8   *everything returns to its roots;*

9   *matter returns to the origins of matter.*

10 *Those who have ears, let them hear."*

11 *Peter said to him: "Since you have become the interpreter*

12 *of the elements and the events of the world, tell us:*

13 *What is the sin of the world?"*

14 *The Teacher answered:*

15 *"There is no sin.*

16 *It is you who make sin exist,*

17 *when you act according to the habits*

18 *of your corrupted nature;*

19 *this is where sin lies.*

20 *This is why the Good has come into your midst.*

21 *It acts together with the elements of your nature*

22 *so as to reunite it with its roots."*

23 *Then he continued:*

24 *"This is why you become sick,*

25 *and why you die:*

26 *it is the result of your actions;*

27 *what you do takes you further away.*

28 *Those who have ears, let them hear.*

[H̄]

ⲙ̅ⲡⲉⲧⲁⲣ̅·ⲡⲁ̣[± 7 ⲡ]ⲉ̣ⲧ[ⲣ̄]
ⲛⲟⲓ̈ ⲙⲁⲣⲉϥⲣ̅ⲛⲟⲉⲓ [ⲁⲑ]ⲩ̣ⲗ̣ⲏ [ⲭⲡ]ⲉ̣ ⲟⲩ
ⲡⲁⲑⲟⲥ ⲉⲙⲛ̅ⲧⲁϥ ⲙⲙⲁⲩ ⲙ̅ⲡⲉⲓⲛⲉ
ⲉⲁϥⲉⲓ ⲉⲃⲟⲗ ϩⲛ ⲟⲩⲡⲁⲣⲁⲫⲩⲥⲓⲥ ⲧⲟ
5   ⲧⲉ ϣⲁⲣⲉⲟⲩⲧⲁⲣⲁⲭⲏ ϣⲱⲡⲉ ϩ̅ⲙ̅
ⲡⲥⲱⲙⲁ ⲧⲏⲣϥ ⲉⲧⲃⲉ ⲡⲁⲓ̈ ⲁⲓ̈ϫⲟⲥ ⲛⲏ
ⲧⲛ̅ ϫⲉ ϣⲱⲡⲉ ⲉⲧⲉⲧⲛ̅ⲧⲏⲧ ⲛ̅ϩⲏⲧ
ⲁⲩⲱ ⲉⲧⲉⲧⲛ̅ⲟ ⲛ̅ⲛⲁⲧⲧⲱⲧ ⲉⲧⲉ
ⲧⲛ̅ⲧⲏⲧ ⲙⲉⲛ ⲛ̅ⲛⲁϩⲣ̅ⲙ̅ ⲡⲓⲛⲉ ⲡⲓⲛⲉ
10   ⲛ̅ⲧⲉⲫⲩⲥⲓⲥ ⲡⲉⲧⲉ ⲟⲩⲛ ⲙⲁⲁϫⲉ ⲙ̅
ⲙⲟϥ ⲉⲥⲱⲧ̅ⲙ̅ ⲙⲁⲣⲉϥⲥⲱⲧ̅ⲙ̅ ⲛ̅ⲧⲁ
ⲣⲉϥϫⲉ ⲛⲁⲓ̈ ⲛ̅ϭⲓ ⲡⲙⲁⲕⲁⲣⲓⲟⲥ ⲁϥⲁⲥ
ⲡⲁϫⲉ ⲙ̅ⲙⲟⲟⲩ ⲧⲏⲣⲟⲩ̀ ⲉϥϫⲱ ⲙ̅ⲙⲟ̀ⲥ̀
ϫⲉ ⲟⲩⲉⲓⲣⲏⲛⲏ ⲛⲏⲧⲛ̅ ⲧⲁⲉⲓⲣⲏⲛⲏ
15   ϫⲡⲟⲥ ⲛⲏⲧⲛ̅ ⲁⲣⲉϩ ⲙ̅ⲡⲣ̅ⲧⲣⲉⲗⲁⲁⲩ ⲣ̅
ⲡⲗⲁⲛⲁ ⲙⲙⲱⲧⲛ̅ ⲉϥϫⲱ ⲙⲙⲟⲥ ϫⲉ
ⲉⲓⲥ ϩⲏⲡⲉ ⲙⲡⲉⲓ̈ⲥⲁ ⲏ̣ ⲉⲓⲥ ϩⲏⲡⲉ ⲙ̅
ⲡⲉⲉⲓⲙⲁ ⲡϣⲏⲣⲉ ⲅⲁⲣ ⲙⲡⲣⲱⲙⲉ ⲉϥ
ϣⲟⲡ ⲙⲡⲉⲧⲛ̅ϩⲟⲩⲛ ⲟⲩⲉϩⲧⲏⲩⲧⲛ̅
20   ⲛ̅ⲥⲱϥ ⲛⲉⲧϣⲓⲛⲉ ⲛ̅ⲥⲱϥ ⲥⲉⲛⲁ
ϭⲛ̅ⲧϥ̅ ⲃⲱⲕ ϭⲉ ⲛ̅ⲧⲉⲧⲛ̅ⲧⲁϣⲉⲟⲉⲓϣ
ⲙⲡⲉⲩⲁⲅⲅⲉⲗⲓⲟⲛ ⲛ̅ⲧⲙⲛ̅ⲧⲉⲣⲟ ⲙⲡⲣ̅

[Page 8]

1   *"Attachment to matter*

2   *gives rise to passion against nature.*

3   *Thus trouble arises in the whole body;*

4   *this is why I tell you:*

5   *'Be in harmony . . .'*

6   *If you are out of balance,*

7   *take inspiration from manifestations*

8   *of your true nature.*

9   *Those who have ears,*

10   *let them hear."*

11   *After saying this, the Blessed One*

12   *greeted them all, saying:*

13   *"Peace be with you—may my Peace*

14   *arise and be fulfilled within you!*

15   *Be vigilant, and allow no one to mislead you*

16   *by saying:*

17   *'Here it is!' or*

18   *'There it is!'*

19   *For it is within you*

20   *that the Son of Man dwells.*

21   *Go to him,*

22   *for those who seek him, find him.*

23   *Walk forth,*

24   *and announce the gospel of the Kingdom."*

[—]
ⲑ̄

ⲕⲁ ⲗⲁⲩ ⲛ̄ϩⲟⲣⲟⲥ ⲉϩⲣⲁⲓ̈ ⲡⲁⲣⲁ ⲡⲉⲛ
ⲧⲁⲓ̈ⲧⲟϣϥ̄ ⲛⲏⲧⲛ̄ ⲟⲩⲇⲉ ⲙ̄ⲡⲣ̄ϯ ⲛⲟ
ⲙⲟⲥ ⲛ̄ⲑⲉ ⲙⲡⲛⲟⲙⲟⲑⲉⲧⲏⲥ ⲙⲏⲡⲟ
ⲧⲉ ⲛ̄ⲥⲉⲁⲙⲁϩⲧⲉ ⲙ̄ⲙⲱⲧⲛ̄ ⲛϩⲏⲧϥ
5   ⲛⲧⲁⲣⲉϥϫⲉ ⲛⲁⲓ̈ ⲁϥⲃⲱⲕ ⲛⲧⲟⲟⲩ ⲇⲉ
ⲛⲉⲩⲣ̄ⲗⲩⲡⲉⲓ ⲁⲩⲣⲓⲙⲉ ⲙ̄ⲡϣⲁ ⲉⲩ
ϫⲱ ⲙⲙⲟⲥ ϫⲉ ⲛⲛⲁϣ ⲛ̄ϩⲉ ⲉⲛⲛⲁⲃⲱⲕ
ϣⲁ ⲛϩⲉⲑⲛⲟⲥ ⲛ̄ⲧⲛ̄ⲧⲁϣⲉⲟⲉⲓϣ ⲛ̄
ⲡⲉⲩⲁⲅⲅⲉⲗⲓⲟⲛ ⲛⲧⲙⲛ̄ⲧⲉⲣⲟ ⲙⲡϣ̄ⲏ′
10   ⲣⲉ ⲙⲡⲣⲱⲙⲉ ⲉϣϫⲉ ⲡⲉⲧⲙ̄ⲙⲁⲩ ⲙ̄
ⲡⲟⲩϯⲥⲟ ⲉⲣⲟϥ ⲛⲁϣ ⲛ̄ϩⲉ ⲁⲛⲟⲛ ⲉⲩ
ⲛⲁϯⲥⲟ ⲉⲣⲟⲛ ⲧⲟⲧⲉ ⲁⲙⲁⲣⲓϩⲁⲙ ⲧⲱ
ⲟⲩⲛ ⲁⲥⲁⲥⲡⲁϩⲉ ⲙⲙⲟⲟⲩ ⲧⲏⲣⲟⲩ
ⲡⲉϫⲁⲥ ⲛⲛⲉⲥ′ⲥ′ⲛⲏⲩ ϫⲉ ⲙⲡⲣ̄ⲣⲓⲙⲉ
15   ⲁⲩⲱ ⲙⲡⲣⲣⲗⲩⲡⲉⲓ ⲟⲩⲇⲉ ⲙ̄ⲡⲣⲣ ϩⲏⲧ
ⲥⲛⲁⲩ ⲧⲉϥⲭⲁⲣⲓⲥ ⲅⲁⲣ ⲛⲁϣⲱⲡⲉ
ⲛⲙ̄ⲙⲏⲧⲛ̄ ⲧⲏⲣ⟨ⲧ⟩ⲛ̣ ⲁⲩⲱ ⲛⲥⲣ̄ⲥⲕⲉⲡⲁ
ϩⲉ ⲙⲙⲱⲧⲛ̄ ⲙⲁⲗⲗⲟⲛ ⲇⲉ ⲙⲁⲣⲛ̄
ⲥⲙⲟⲩ ⲉⲧⲉϥⲙⲛ̄ⲧⲛⲟϭ ϫⲉ ⲁϥⲥ̄ⲃ
20   ⲧⲱⲧⲛ̄ ⲁϥⲁⲁⲛ ⲛ̄ⲣⲱⲙⲉ ⲛⲧⲁⲣⲉⲙⲁ
ⲣⲓϩⲁⲙ ϫⲉ ⲛⲁⲓ̈ ⲁⲥⲕⲧⲉ ⲡⲉⲩϩⲏⲧ
[ⲉϩ]ⲟⲩⲛ ⲉⲡⲁⲅⲁⲑⲟⲛ ⲁⲩⲱ ⲁⲩⲣ̄ⲁⲣⲭⲉ
[ⲥⲑⲁⲓ] ⲛ̣ⲣ̄ⲅⲩⲙ[ⲛ]ⲁ̣ϩⲉ ϩⲁ ⲡⲣⲁ ⲛⲛ̄ϣⲁ
[ϫ]ⲉ ⲙⲡ̄[ⲥⲱⲣ]

[Page 9]

1   *"Impose no law*

2   *other than that which I have witnessed.*

3   *Do not add more laws to those given in the Torah,*

4   *lest you become bound by them."*

5   *Having said all this, he departed.*

6   *The disciples were in sorrow,*

7   *shedding many tears, and saying:*

8   *"How are we to go among the unbelievers*

9   *and announce the gospel of the Kingdom of the Son of Man?*

10   *They did not spare his life,*

11   *so why should they spare ours?"*

12   *Then Mary arose,*

13   *embraced them all, and began to speak to her brothers:*

14   *"Do not remain in sorrow and doubt,*

15   *for his Grace will guide you and comfort you.*

16   *Instead, let us praise his greatness,*

17   *for he has prepared us for this.*

18   *He is calling upon us to become fully human [Anthropos]."* [30]

19   *Thus Mary turned their hearts toward the Good,*

20   *and they began to discuss the meaning of the Teacher's words.*

---

[30][*Anthropos* is the original Greek word used. Leloup's inclusion of this word here is to indicate that our impoverished modern word *human* (*humains*, in French) cannot be an adequate translation.—*Trans.*]

ī

πεχε πετρος ммαριзαм χε τcω
νε τ̄ncooγn χε νερεπcω̄ρ oγαϣε
nзoγo παρα πκεcεεπε nc̄зїμε
χω nαn ñnϣαχε μ̄πcω̄ρ ετεειρε
5 μπεγμεεγε nαϊ ετεcooγn μ̄μo
oγ ñnαnon αn oγδε μπ̄ncoτμ`oγ
αcoγωϣβ ñϭι μαριзαμ πεχαc
χε πεθηπ ερωτ̄n †nαταμα τηγ
τ̄n εροч αγω αcαρχει ñχω nαγ
10 ñnεϊϣαχε χε αϊnoκ πεχαc αι
nαγ επ̄χc̄ зn oγзoρoμα αγω αει
χooc nαч χε π̄χc̄ αϊnαγ εροκ μ̄
πooγ зn oγзoρoμα αчoγωϣβ πε
χαч nαϊ χε nαϊατε χε ñτεκιμ αn
15 ερεnαγ εροει πμα γαρ ετερεπnoγc
μ̄μαγ εчμμαγ ñϭι πεзo πεχαϊ
nαч χε π̄χc̄ τεnoγ πετnαγ εφo
ρoμα εчnαγ εροч⟨зñ⟩τεψγχη ⟨η⟩
πεπn̄ᾱ αчoγωϣβ ñϭι πcω̄ρ πε
20 χαч χε εчnαγ αn зñ τεψγχη oγ
δε зμ πεπn̄ᾱ αλλα πnoγc ετϣ[oπ]
зn τεγμητε μπεγϭnαγ ñτo[ч πετ]
nαγ εφoρoμα αγ[ω] ñτoч π̄[ετ...]

[Page 10]

1   Peter said to Mary:

2   "Sister, we know that the Teacher loved you

3   differently from other women.

4   Tell us whatever you remember

5   of any words he told you

6   which we have not yet heard."

7   Mary said to them:

8   "I will now speak to you

9   of that which has not been given to you to hear.

10   I had a vision of the Teacher,

11   and I said to him:

12   'Lord I see you now

13   in this vision.'

14   And he answered:

15   'You are blessed, for the sight of me does not disturb you.

16   There where is the nous, lies the treasure.'

17   Then I said to him:

18   'Lord, when someone meets you

19   in a Moment of vision,

20   is it through the soul [psyche] that they see,

21   or is it through the Spirit [Pneuma] ?'

22   The Teacher answered:

23   'It is neither through the soul nor the spirit,

24   but the nous between the two

25   which sees the vision, and it is this which [. . .]' "

ⲙⲙⲟϥ ⲁⲩⲱ ⲡⲉϫⲉ ⲧⲉⲡⲓⲑⲩⲙⲓⲁ
ϫⲉ ⲙⲡⲓⲛⲁⲩ ⲉⲣⲟ ⲉⲣⲉⲃⲏⲕ ⲉⲡⲓⲧⲛ̄
ⲧⲉⲛⲟⲩ ⲇⲉ ϯⲛⲁⲩ ⲉⲣⲟ ⲉⲣⲉⲃⲏⲕ ⲉ
ⲧⲡⲉ ⲡⲱⲥ ⲇⲉ ⲧⲉϫⲓ ⲃⲟⲗ ⲉⲣⲉⲛⲡ' ⲉ
5 ⲣⲟⲉⲓ ⲁⲥⲟⲩⲱϣⲃ̄ ⲛ̄ϭⲓ ⲧⲉⲯⲩⲭⲏ ⲡⲉ
ϫⲁⲥ ϫⲉ ⲁⲓ̈ⲛⲁⲩ ⲉⲣⲟ ⲙⲡⲉⲛⲁⲩ ⲉⲣⲟⲓ̈
ⲟⲩⲇⲉ ⲙⲡⲉⲉⲓⲙⲉ ⲉⲣⲟⲉⲓ ⲛⲉⲉⲓϣⲟ
ⲟⲡ ⲛⲉ ⲛ̄ϩⲃⲥⲱ ⲁⲩⲱ ⲙⲡⲉⲥⲟⲩⲱⲛⲧ
ⲛ̄ⲧⲁⲣⲉⲥϫⲉ ⲛⲁⲓ̈ ⲁⲥⲃⲱⲕ ⲉⲥⲧⲉⲗⲏⲗ
10 ⲛ̄ϩⲟⲩⲟ ⟩ ⲡⲁⲗⲓⲛ ⲁⲥⲉⲓ ⲉⲧⲛ̄ ⲧⲙⲉϩ
ϣⲟⲙⲛⲧⲉ ⲛ̄ⲛⲉϫⲟⲩⲥⲓⲁ ⲧⲉⲧⲟⲩⲙ'ⲟ'ⲩ
ⲧⲉ ⲉⲣⲟⲥ ϫⲉ ⲧⲙⲛ̄ⲧⲁⲧⲥⲟⲟⲩⲛ [ⲁⲥ]ⲣ̄
ⲉϫⲉⲧⲁϫⲉ ⲛ̄ⲧⲉⲯⲩⲭⲏ ⲉⲥϫ[ⲱ ⲙ]
ⲙⲟⲥ ϫⲉ ⲉⲣⲉⲃⲏⲕ ⲉⲧⲱⲛ ϩⲛ̄ [ⲟ]ⲩⲡⲟ̄
15 ⲛⲏⲣⲓⲁ ⲁⲩⲁⲙⲁϩⲧⲉ ⲙⲙⲟ ⲁⲩ[ⲁ]ⲙⲁ̣ϩ̣
ⲧⲉ ⲇⲉ ⲙⲙⲟ ⲙⲡⲣ̄ⲕⲣⲓⲛⲉ ⲁⲩ[ⲱ] ⲡⲉ
ϫⲉ ⲧⲉⲯⲩⲭⲏ ϫⲉ ⲁϩⲣⲟ ⲉⲣⲉⲕⲣ̣ⲓ̣ⲛ̣ⲉ̣
ⲙⲙⲟⲓ̈ ⲉⲙⲡⲓⲕⲣⲓⲛⲉ ⲁⲩⲉⲙⲁϩⲧⲉ
ⲙⲙⲟⲓ̈ ⲉⲙⲡⲓⲁⲙⲁϩⲧⲉ ⲙⲡⲟⲩϭ̣ⲟ̣ⲩ
20 ⲱⲛⲧ ⲁⲛⲟⲕ ⲇⲉ ⲁⲓ̈ⲥⲟⲩⲱⲛⲟⲩ ⲉⲩ
ⲃⲱⲗ ⲉⲃⲟⲗ ⲙⲡⲧⲏⲣϥ ⲉⲓⲧⲉ ⲛⲁ ⲡ

[Pages 11–14 are missing]

[Page 15]

1   *"And Craving said:*

2   *'I did not see you descend,*

3   *but now I see you rising.*

4   *Why do you lie, since you belong to me?'*

5   *The soul answered:*

6   *'I saw you,*

7   *though you did not see me,*

8   *nor recognize me.*

9   *I was with you as with a garment,*

10   *and you never felt me.'*

11   *Having said this,*

12   *the soul left, rejoicing greatly.*

13   *Then it entered into the third climate,*

14   *known as Ignorance.*

15   *Ignorance inquired of the soul:*

16   *'Where are you going?*

17   *You are dominated by wicked inclinations.*

18   *Indeed, you lack discrimination, and you are enslaved.'*

19   *The soul answered:*

20   *'Why do you judge me, since I have made no judgment?*

21   *I have been dominated, but I myself have not dominated.*

22   *I have not been recognized,*

23   *but I myself have recognized*

24   *that all things which are composed shall be decomposed,*

25   *on earth and in heaven.'"*

ειτε να τπ[ε] ῆτερετεψγχη ογ
ωϲϥ ῆτμεϩϣομντε ῆνεϩογϲι
α αϲβωκ επϲα ντπε αγω αϲναγ
ετμαϩϥτοε ῆνεϩογϲια αϲⲣ̄ ϲα
5 ϣϥε νῆμορφη τϣορπ ῆμορ
φη πε πκακε τμεϩϲῆτε τεπι
θγμια τμεϩϣομντε τμῆτατ
ϲοογν τμεϩϥτοε πε πκωϩ ῆπ
μογ τμεϩϯε τε τμῆτερο ῆτϲαρϩ
10 τμεϩϲοε τε τμῆτϲαβη νϲεβη
ῆϲαρϩ τμεϩϲαϣϥε τε τϲοφι
α [ν]ρεϥνογϭϲ ναϊ νε τϲαϣϥε ῆ
νε[ϩ]ογϲια ντε τοργη εγϣινε
ῆτεψγχη χε ερεννγ χιν των
15 τϩατβρωμε η ερεβηκ ετων
τογαϲϥμα αϲογωϣⲃ̄ ῆϭι τε
ψγχη πεχαϲ χε πετεμαϩτε ῆ
μοϊ αγκονϲϥ̄ αγω πεκτο ῆ
μοϊ αγογοϲϥ αγω ταεπιθγμια
20 αϲχωκ εβολ αγω τμῆτατϲοογ̄
αϲμογ ˙ϩῆ˙ ογⲕ̣οⲥ̣μοϲ ῆταγβολτˏ ε

[Page 16]

1   *"Freed from this third climate, the soul continued its ascent,*

2   *and found itself in the fourth climate.*

3   *This has seven manifestations:*

4   *the first manifestation is Darkness;*

5   *the second, Craving;*

6   *the third, Ignorance;*

7   *the fourth, Lethal Jealousy;*

8   *the fifth, Enslavement to the Body;*

9   *the sixth, Intoxicated Wisdom;*

10   *the seventh, Guileful Wisdom.*

11   *These are the seven manifestations of Wrath,*

12   *and they oppressed the soul with questions:*

13   *'Where do you come from, murderer?'*

14   *and 'Where are you going, vagabond?'*

15   *The soul answered:*

16   *'That which oppressed me has been slain;*

17   *that which encircled me has vanished;*

18   *my craving has faded,*

19   *and I am freed from my ignorance.'"*

ιζ

βολ ₂ⲚⲚ ογκοϲⲙοϲ [αγ]ω ₂Ⲛ ογ
ΤΥⲠΟС ⲈⲂΟⲖ ₂Ⲛ ΟΥΤΥⲠΟС ⲈΤⲘ
ⲠⲤⲀ ⲚΤⲠⲈ ⲀΥⲰ ΤⲘⲢⲢⲈ ⲚΤⲂ̅ϢⲈ ⲈΤ
ϢΟΟⲠ ⲠⲢΟⲤ ΟΥΟῙϢ ϪΙⲚ Ⲙ̅ⲠⲒⲚⲀΥ
5 ⲈⲈΙⲚⲀϪΙ ⲚΤⲀⲚⲀⲠⲀΥⲤΙⲤ ⲘⲠⲈ
ⲬⲢΟⲚΟⲤ ⲘⲠⲔⲀΙⲢΟⲤ ⲘⲠ'ⲀΙ'ⲰⲚ ₂Ⲛ
ⲚΟΥⲔⲀⲢⲰϥ ⲚΤⲈⲢⲈⲘⲀⲢΙ₂ⲀⲘ ϪⲈ
ⲚⲀῙ ⲀⲤⲔⲀ ⲢⲰⲤ ₂ⲰⲤΤⲈ Ⲛ̅ΤⲀⲠⲤ̅ⲰⲢ̅
ϢⲀⲬⲈ ⲚⲘ̅ⲘⲀⲤ ϢⲀ ⲠⲈⲈΙⲘⲀ
10 ⲀϥΟΥⲰϢⲂ̅ ⲀⲈ Ⲛ̅ϬⲒ ⲀⲚⲆⲢⲈⲀⲤ ⲠⲈϪⲀϥ
Ⲛ̅ⲚⲈⲤⲚⲎΥ ϪⲈ ⲀϪⲒ ⲠⲈΤⲈΤⲚ̅ϪⲰ
ⲘⲘΟϥ ₂Ⲁ ⲠⲢⲀ Ⲛ̅ⲚⲈⲚΤⲀⲤϪ[Ο]ΟΥ
ⲀⲚΟⲔ ⲘⲈⲚ †Ⲣ̅ⲠΙⲤΤⲈΥⲈ ⲀⲚ ϪⲈ
ⲀⲠⲤ̅ⲰⲢ̅ ϪⲈ ⲚⲀῙ ⲈϢϪⲈ ⲚΙⲤⲂΟΟΥ
15 Ⲉ ⲄⲀⲢ ₂Ⲛ̅ⲔⲈⲘⲈⲈΥⲈ ⲚⲈ ⲀϥΟΥⲰ
ϢⲂ̅ Ⲛ̅ϬⲒ ⲠⲈΤⲢΟⲤ ⲠⲈϪⲀϥ ₂Ⲁ ⲠⲢⲀ
ⲚⲚⲈⲈΙ₂ⲂⲎΥⲈ ⲚΤⲈⲈΙⲘΙⲚⲈ Ⲁϥ
ϪⲚΟΥΟΥ ⲈΤⲂⲈ ⲠⲤ̅ⲰⲢ̅ ϪⲈ ⲘⲎΤⲒ
ⲀϥϢⲀⲬⲈ ⲘⲚ̅ ΟΥⲤ₂ῙⲘⲈ ⲚϪΙΟΥⲈ
20 ⲈⲢΟⲚ ₂Ⲛ ΟΥⲰⲚ₂ ⲈⲂΟⲖ ⲀⲚ ⲈⲚⲚⲀ
ⲔΤΟⲚ ₂ⲰⲰⲚ Ⲛ̅ΤⲚ̅ⲤⲰΤⲘ̅ ΤⲎⲢⲚ̅
ⲚⲤⲰⲤ Ⲛ̅Τ<Ⲁ>ϥⲤΟΤⲠⲤ Ⲛ₂ΟΥΟ ⲈⲢΟⲚ

[Page 17]

1   *" I left the world with the aid of another world;*

2   *a design was erased,*

3   *by virtue of a higher design.*

4   *Henceforth I travel toward Repose,*

5   *where time rests in the Eternity of Time;*

6   *I go now into Silence.'"*

7   *Having said all this, Mary became silent,*

8   *for it was in silence that the Teacher spoke to her.*

9   *Then Andrew began to speak, and said to his brothers:*

10 *"Tell me, what do you think of these things she has been*
telling us?

11 *As for me, I do not believe*

12 *that the Teacher would speak like this.*

13 *These ideas are too different from those we have*
known."

14 *And Peter added:*

15 *"How is it possible that the Teacher talked*

16 *in this manner with a woman*

17 *about secrets of which we ourselves are ignorant?*

18 *Must we change our customs,*

19 *and listen to this woman?*

20 *Did he really choose her, and prefer her to us?"*

$\overline{\text{IH}}$

ⲧⲟⲧⲉ ⲁ[ⲙ]ⲁⲣⲓϩⲁⲙ ⲣⲓⲙⲉ ⲡⲉⲭⲁⲥ ⲙ̄
ⲡⲉⲧⲣⲟⲥ ⟨ⲭⲉ⟩ ⲡⲁⲥⲟⲛ ⲡⲉⲧⲣⲉ ϩⲓ̈ⲉ ⲉⲕ
ⲙⲉⲉⲩⲉ ⲉⲟⲩ ⲉⲕⲙⲉⲉⲩⲉ ⲭⲉ ⲛ̄ⲧⲁⲓ̈
ⲙⲉⲉⲩⲉ ⲉⲣⲟⲟⲩ ⲙⲁⲩⲁⲁⲧ ϩⲙ̄ ⲡⲁ
5 ϩⲏⲧ ⲏ ⲉⲉⲓⲭⲓ ⲃⲟⲗ ⲉⲡⲥⲱⲣ ⲁϥⲟⲩ
ⲱϣⲃ̄ ⲛ̄ϭⲓ ⲗⲉⲅⲉⲓ ⲡⲉⲭⲁϥ ⲙⲡⲉⲧⲣⲟʼⲥʼ
ⲭⲉ ⲡⲉⲧⲣⲉ ⲭⲓⲛ ⲉⲛⲉϩ ⲕϣⲟⲡ ⲛⲣⲉϥ
ⲛⲟⲩϭⲥ ⲧ̄ⲛⲁⲩ ⲉⲣⲟⲕ ⲧⲉⲛⲟⲩ ⲉⲕⲣ̄
ⲅⲩⲙⲛⲁⲍⲉ ⲉϩⲛ ⲧⲉⲥϩⲓ̈ⲙⲉ ⲛ̄ⲑⲉ ⲛ̄
10 ⲛⲓⲁⲛⲧⲓⲕⲉⲓⲙⲉⲛⲟⲥ ⲉϣⲭⲉ ⲁⲡ
ⲥⲱⲧⲏⲣ ⲇⲉ ⲁⲁⲥ ⲛⲁϩⲓⲟⲥ ⲛ̄ⲧⲕ ⲛⲓⲙ
ⲇⲉ ϩⲱⲱⲕ ⲉⲛⲟⲭⲥ ⲉⲃⲟⲗ ⲡⲁⲛⲧⲱʼⲥʼ
ⲉⲣⲉⲡⲥⲱⲧⲏⲣ ⲥⲟⲟⲩⲛ ⲙ̄ⲙⲟⲥ ⲁⲥ
ⲫⲁⲗⲱⲥ ⲉⲧⲃⲉ ⲡⲁⲓ̈ ⲁϥⲟⲩⲟϣⲥ̄ ⲛ̄ϩⲟⲩ
15 ⲟ ⲉⲣⲟⲛ ⲙⲁⲗⲗⲟⲛ ⲙⲁⲣⲛ̄ϣⲓⲡⲉ ⲛ̄ⲧⲛ
ⲧ ϩⲓ̈ⲱⲱⲛ ⲙⲡⲣⲱⲙⲉ ⲛ̄ⲧⲉⲗⲓⲟⲥ
ⲛ̄ⲧⲛ̄ⲭⲡⲟϥ ⲛ̄ⲁⲛ ⲕⲁⲧⲁ ⲑⲉ ⲛ̄ⲧⲁϥ
ϩⲱⲛ ⲉⲧⲟⲟⲧⲛ̄ ⲛ̄ⲧⲛ̄ⲧⲁϣⲉⲟⲉⲓϣ
ⲙⲡⲉⲩⲁⲅⲅⲉⲗⲓⲟⲛ ⲉⲛⲕⲱ ⲁⲛ ⲉϩⲣⲁⲓ̈
20 ⲛ̄ⲕⲉϩⲟⲣⲟⲥ ⲟⲩⲇⲉ ⲕⲉⲛⲟⲙⲟⲥ ⲡⲁ
ⲣⲁ ⲡⲉⲛⲧⲁⲡⲥⲱⲣ ⲭⲟⲟϥ ⲛ̄ⲧⲉⲣⲉ

[Page 18]

1   *Then Mary wept,*

2   *and answered him:*

3   *"My brother Peter, what can you be thinking?*

4   *Do you believe that this is just my own imagination,*

5   *that I invented this vision?*

6   *Or do you believe that I would lie about our Teacher?"*

7   *At this, Levi spoke up:*

8   *"Peter, you have always been hot-tempered,*

9   *and now we see you repudiating a woman,*

10   *just as our adversaries do.*

11   *Yet if the Teacher held her worthy,*

12   *who are you to reject her?*

13   *Surely the Teacher knew her very well,*

14   *for he loved her more than us.*

15   *Therefore let us atone,*

16   *and become fully human [Anthropos],*

17   *so that the Teacher can take root in us.*

18   *Let us grow as he demanded of us,*

19   *and walk forth to spread the gospel,*

20   *without trying to lay down any rules and laws*

21   *other than those he witnessed."*

[ī]ē

[ⲗⲉ]ⲅ[ⲉⲓ ⲇⲉ ϫⲉ ⲛ]ⲁ̈ⲓ ⲁⲩⲱ ⲁⲅⲣⲁⲣⲭⲉⲓ ⲛ̄
ⲃⲱⲕ [ⲉⲧⲣⲉⲩⲧ]ⲁⲙⲟ ⲛ̄ⲥⲉⲧⲁϣⲉⲟⲉⲓϣ
ⲡ[ⲉ]ⲩⲁⲅⲅⲉⲗⲓⲟⲛ

⌣ⲕⲁⲧⲁ⌣

ⲙⲁⲣⲓ̇ϩⲁⲙⲙ

[Page 19]

1 *When Levi had said these words,*

2 *they all went forth to spread the gospel.*

3 THE GOSPEL

   ACCORDING TO

   MARY

PART TWO

Text with Commentary

[Pages 1–6 are missing.]

[Page 7]

1   [. . .] *"What is matter?*

2   *Will it last forever?"*

3   *The Teacher answered:*

4   *"All that is born, all that is created,*

5   *all the elements of nature*

6   *are interwoven and united with each other.*

7   *All that is composed shall be decomposed;*

8   *everything returns to its roots;*

9   *matter returns to the origins of matter.*

10   *Those who have ears, let them hear."*

" . . . What is matter?" Before asking questions about the meaning, purpose, or workings of the world, it is appropriate to inquire into what it
really is, and if it was made to last or not. "Will it last forever?"—might it
not be an illusion?

With the Gospel of Mary, it is clear from the start that we are dealing with a deeply metaphysical perspective. Prior to any questions about
our actions and their rightness or wrongness, it is important to ask *if* we
are, and *who* we are. Before we ask the ancient question "Why does the
world contain evil and suffering?"we must first question how we know it
exists at all.

Thus the path of Christianity that we find in this gospel is one of
gnosis, or divine knowledge—it goes deeper than the teaching of rules by
which we can live and improve ourselves. Here, Yeshua has something to
say about the fundamental nature of the world and of humanness.

The Gospel of Mary presents him as the Teacher, and the teaching he
transmits contains the knowledge necessary for the reintegration of
human beings with themselves and with their Source and Principle—the
One that, in most of the gospels, Yeshua calls his Father: "my Father and
your Father," and "my God and your God," as he tells Mary Magdalene

in John 20:17. These are the teachings that can restore human beings to their lost parentage, to an indescribably singular intimacy with their Source. Yeshua has always lived in this intimacy, and his words and actions are the expression and manifestation of it.

Some translators of this gospel have rendered the word for teacher as *savior.* This is another possibility, but only if we bear in mind that what people really need to be saved from is their ignorance and forgetfulness of the Being that is their source and destination. Human beings are to be saved from their ignorance and obliviousness of the Presence that Yeshua embodies. First and foremost, *salvation* is knowledge of the truth that shall make us free—free of attachments and identifications with that which we mistake for real Being. In these verses, it is matter that is taken as an example of this.

> *The Teacher answered:*
> *"All that is born, all that is created,*
> *all the elements of nature*
> *are interwoven and united with each other.*
> *All that is composed shall be decomposed;"*

This reminder of the interdependence and impermanence of all things is striking in its resonance with contemporary thinking: Nothing exists in itself or by itself, for the world is a vast tapestry woven of relations. Not even the smallest strand in this web can be tugged without affecting all the myriad strands and interdependencies to which it is connected, and of which it is composed. This is true of matter, and it is also true of the nature of the human body and the psyche that animates it.

Everything that exists is a more or less complex pattern of components, and is therefore subject to decomposition: "All that is composed shall be decomposed." This is a truth that reminds us that this universe we perceive has not always existed, and that it will not exist forever. What has a beginning also has an end. Ignorance of impermanence generates illusions, attachments, and therefore suffering—all the ancient wisdom traditions tell us this.

For "those who have ears" capable of hearing this word of the Teacher, this can be a source of salvation and freedom. No longer do we continue to indulge in the idolatry of matter. This appreciation of the ephemeral and relative nature of all things actually enables us to love better—we begin to see all things with that loving yet detached regard and equanimity that are the signs of a genuine health of soul. In Greek, the word *soteria* means both "health" (wholeness) and "salvation."

The Teacher then adds:

> *"everything returns to its roots;*
> *matter returns to the origins of matter."*

All evolution involves a return; yet a return in this sense is not the same as a regression. To return is not to go back—rather, the return is accomplished by moving forward. It is a return to the place that is both our origin and our destiny, our alpha and our omega. Here we make an important distinction between the Origin, or the Source, and the beginning. We return to the Source, not to our beginning.

Furthermore, the Kingdom that is spoken of in the Gospel of Mary[31] must not be confused with a return to some sort of lost paradise or primal state of consciousness. Rather, it signifies an awakening to this very dimension of Being that is the source of our existence now, and of the mystery of there being *something* instead of *nothing*.

A grain of wheat contains the information that will later generate roots, stem, leaves, and finally the new grains, which ripen slowly with sun and rain and finally offer themselves to the nourishment of those who eat them.

Then comes winter, decay, and the new planting of the grain— returning to the roots, yet also to the root symbolized by the information

---

[31][This also applies to the sense of the Kingdom in the Gospel of Thomas 113: His disciples said to him, "When will the kingdom come?"

"It will not come by watching for it. It will not be said, 'Behold, here!' or 'Behold, there!' Rather, the Father's kingdom is spread out upon the earth, and people do not see it."—*Trans.*]

in the grain. But the true Source cannot be grasped by the mind, though it is the source of the mind and of all things. Thus "matter returns to the origins of matter." Yet the ultimate Source can never be an object of any kind, and can only appear as nothingness, "Nothing that can be found in the All of which It is the cause."

In speaking of the Logos, the Gospel of John (1:3), which was probably written during the same period, says that:

> *Through Him all things came into being;*
> *Not one thing came into being except through Him.*

The Logos, the Origin, this nothing that is the cause of everything, and through which all things have their being—what are we speaking of when we speak of this divinity as He, She, or It? Surely it is nothing that can be imagined, thought, or represented. Yet if we also subscribe to the principle that nothing comes from nothing, then what can be the meaning of this unthinkable fecundity, this womb of emptiness?

"Those who have ears, let them hear." This recurrent phrase is not some elitist irony through which the Teacher alludes to secret tidbits; nor does it reflect an impatience with long explanations. It is an invitation to "have ears," to develop an organ of subtle perception, a special faculty of attention. We are not yet speaking of the visionary nous of the following verses, but of the contemplative intelligence that arises from endless wonder at all Being, a kind of feeling for the infinite open, without which the unveiling of true being is impossible. For the Real only offers itself to those who take the time needed to *hear*, those who can endure and listen fully to the silence of the fathomless before it finally begins to speak.

Shema Yisraël—"Listen O Israel!" The same practice that Moses advocated to his distracted, chattering companions is the one transmitted through this teaching of Yeshua:

If the conscious subject has no ears
there will be nothing to hear;
if the eyes are not open
there will be nothing to see;
if the heart or the nous is not awake,
there will be nothing to understand . . .

Matter and its origins will offer them neither obscurity, nor clarity, nor meaning.[32]

[Page 7, continued]

11   *Peter said to him: "Since you have become the interpreter*
12   *of the elements and the events of the world, tell us:*
13   *What is the sin of the world?"*
14   *The Teacher answered:*
15   *"There is no sin.*
16   *It is you who make sin exist,*
17   *when you act according to the habits*
18   *of your corrupted nature;*
19   *this is where sin lies."*

Having listened to the Teacher, and having recognized him as the Interpreter (*hermeneutes*), he who imagines and gives meaning to the elements and events of the world, Peter now questions him, in the language of that period, about "the sin of the world." The meaning of this term is often very unclear—both in Yeshua's time and after, there were those who held that human nature itself is tainted with original sin, that matter, the world, and the body are traps from which deliverance is needed. When one sees sin and evil everywhere, the consequences are especially serious

---

[32]A sweeping eschatological interpretation is also possible for verses 7–10. Just as Matthew tells us that not "one stone upon another" will remain of the material edifice of the Temple, since "all shall be dissolved" (*kataluthéstai*, in Greek—Mt. 24:2) from roof to foundation, so these lines could be interpreted as saying that the elements of the entire material universe "shall be dissolved" *(euna bôl ebol)*.

when they are seen as being in an "other," for this other must then be destroyed or killed. Those who have committed such crimes in the name of the Good see themselves not as murderers, but as saviors, ridding the world of sin and evil so as to make it pure again.

All such persecutions, bans, burnings at the stake, and death camps are founded upon the same logic: The rotten apple must be removed from the barrel to rid the whole contents of contamination. All the "rotten" humans who trouble the corridors of power of the "prince of this world" must be liquidated in order to have an uncontaminated society. This is easily extended to whole groups or races of people who embody the evil—otherwise, they will destroy us first. There is nothing new under the sun about this, for the monstrous banality of such thinking is still with us today, just as it was in early Christian times.

These mechanisms tend to repeat themselves, so that when they carry the day, our present seems to be no more than the accumulation of our past. The new teaching has still not been heard. Yet the word of the Teacher here is unmistakably clear in the way it cuts through this question:

> *"There is no sin.*
> *It is you who make sin exist . . ."*

There are of course different levels of interpretation of this. Let us begin with the traditional reading, and see how it opens naturally into a deeper interpretation. It might be summarized as: "There is no sin, only sinners." Matter, the world, the body, are not sinful in and of themselves—yet it is possible to make bad use of them, and we are all more or less sinners to the degree that we do not know how to adjust or harmonize ourselves with the Real. Instead of experiencing peace, we not only hit the wrong notes, but we create shrill disharmony and war.

Nevertheless, it is clear that matter is not bad, nor is anything that exists in the world—in fact, neither the body nor sexuality are bad or sinful. Echoes of the above passage can even be heard in the writings of Paul—for instance, in this extract from his letter to Titus (1:15): "All is pure to those who are pure. But nothing is pure to those who are con-taminated and do not believe."

The meaning of Paul's words is this: It is you who have made sin exist.

Thus sin is not inherent in things, nor is it some element of the cos-mos, nor of human nature. Yet it is definitely found in the way human nature is translated. It is a disorientation of desire, a kind of overlooking or missing the goal. And here Yeshua's word rejoins the etymology of the Greek word for sin—*hamartia*, "to miss the mark."

Through poor use of our senses, intelligence, and emotions, these faculties have become disoriented—they have lost their *orient,* that is to say, their attunement with the Being that is at the heart of all the imper-manent, transitory phenomena of the world. It is only this dis-orientation that enables us to pervert ourselves, society, and the universal order itself.

As was said in the introduction, the only sin is that which we create with our sickly imagination. It is this imagination—or rather, impover-ishment of imagination—that needs to be healed. We are responsible for the world in which we live, for in a deep sense it is we who create it by interpreting it positively or negatively. Our lack of enlightened imagina-tion encloses the world in "being-for-death,"[33] and encloses us in an arrested perception of the world. Our sickness is that we continually take our relative perceptions as absolutely real. We mistake our interpretations and readings of reality for Reality itself. This is where illusion, or sin, lies, according to the Teacher:

> *"It is you who make sin exist,*
> *when you act according to the habits*
> *of your corrupted nature;*
> *this is where sin lies."*

---

[33][A term sometimes used in Heideggerian discourse, *being-for-death* refers to the way of living and being that makes an individual a prisoner of linear, chronological, passing time, thus blocking him from experiencing life as more than a linear sequence with a terminus or outcome that is death.—*Trans.*]

Now, what does it mean, "to act according to the habits of our corrupted nature?" First, it is acting according to modes of thought that have become what common language calls *second nature*—another nature that has been superimposed upon our true and "innocent" condition, a covering made up of projections, a priori assumptions, and judgments that are more or less inherited from others. We apply these automatically and without the slightest concern for any examination or verification that might help us to find out whether this prism through which we decipher reality is really telling us about Reality, or on the contrary, hiding it from us: "You see the splinter in the eye of your neighbor, but you do not see the log in your own."[34]

It is obvious that the word *corrupted* as used here has no sexual connotation. As in the Bible, corruption is related to the deeper meaning of idolatry: taking as Real that which is merely relative or, as Kierkegaard said, making the relative absolute, and making the absolute relative. In other words, the dramatic "sin" of the contemporary world[35] is its relativizing of the absolute, and its absolutizing of the relative. It is hard to imagine a better description of the nature of corruption.

This is a sickness of the intelligence as well as of the heart. It *espouses* its perceptions as Truth, thereby betraying both Truth and itself. One of the most painful consequences of this short-sightedness, this disorientation of desire, is taking yourself for what you are not, indentifying yourself with an image. This is typically a representation derived (whether positively or negatively) from one that our parents or our peers may have of us. The pathologies that are known nowadays as inflation, megalomania, manic-depressive swings, etc., are but extreme forms of this condition.

It is interesting to note several correspondences between these passages and chapter 7 of Paul's Epistle to the Romans. This theme will be explored in more depth later, when we examine the Teacher's words that urge us not to invent more laws—for where there is no law, there is no sin. As with Paul, "without the law, sin is dead" and corruption is no more. In

---

[34]Mt 7:3; Lk 6:41; the Gospel of Thomas 26.

[35]Again, in its original Greek sense of *hamartia*, "missing the mark."

contrast to this, those who invent laws also make sin exist. Of course laws surely do have a pedagogical function, and in early stages of spiritual and physical development it would be dangerous to do without them. A baby who eats food that is too solid will become ill (to use a metaphor of which Paul is fond). But for an adult, things are not the same. The Gospel of Mary is addressed to adults who have integrated the law in themselves. For them, the law is no longer a barrier to the movement of life and the inspirations of the Spirit—like the wind, it fills the sails of their truest desires and calls them to the freedom of open spaces. (In Hebrew, to be saved is to "breathe freely.")

Let us now examine these parallels between Paul's Epistle to the Romans and the Gospel of Mary. The following table will serve to show the correlation of several themes in Romans with those of Mary 7:11–19, and will also prepare us for the later commentary regarding Mary 9:2–4.

COMMON THEMES	ROMANS 7	GOSPEL OF MARY
Corrupt or *adulterous union,* which falls under the authority of the Law	Example of the woman who can no longer be considered an adulteress, because she is free from the Law: " . . . but if her husband be dead, *she is free from that law; so that she is no adultress,* though she be married to another man." (Rom 7:2)	" . . . when you act according to the habits of your *corrupted* nature." (Mary 7:16–18)
(belonging to the Resurrected One)	Wherefore, my brothers, you "too have died to the Law . . . so as to belong to another, to him who has raised from the dead." (Rom 7:3–4)	The disciples are commanded to follow the *Son of Man* without imposing any new Law.

Liberation from the *Law that binds* (enslaves)	"But now we are delivered from the *Law*, for we became dead to that which *bound* us." (Rom 7:6)	"Do not add more *laws* to those given in the Torah [i.e., in the manner of a Legislator], lest you become *bound* by them." (Mary 9:2–4)
Non-existence of sin	"For without the Law, *sin is dead*." (Rom 7:8)	"There is no *sin*. It is you who *make sin exist* . . ." (Mary 7:13–14)
The sequence *Law, sin, death*	" . . . but when the *commandment* came, *sin* came to life, and *I died*." (Rom 7:9–10)	"This is why you become sick, and why you *die*." (Mary 7:21–22)
Two Laws in conflict	"In *my inmost self*, I delight in God's Law; but in my members I perceive another Law which is at war with . . . the Law of my intelligence, and which *holds me captive* to the Law of sin . . ." (Rom 7:22–23)	Two commandments: 1) Follow the *Son of Man*, who dwells *within oneself*; 2) Shun the *Law of the Legislator*, which brings *enslavement*. (Mary 9:2–4; 18:20)

Just as Paul asks that Christians free themselves from the domination of laws (traditional, conscious, and unconscious ones), so as to live through the Spirit of the Resurrection, the Gospel of Mary invites them to live this same freedom by abiding with the One who, in their own inmost being, incarnates all goodness and guides them into the vibrant flow of intimacy with their uncreated Source.

[Page 7, continued]

20   *"This is why the Good has come into your midst.*

21   *It acts together with the elements of your nature*

22   *so as to reunite it with its roots."*

Lack calls for fullness. Thirst calls for the Source. The Good has come into our midst because the nature of matter involves lack. Humans as we know them are beings who feel a lack of Being. The process of corruption begins with their own identification with this lack. They then confuse themselves with the matter of which their bodies are composed, which ultimately leads to an experience of their own vanity and emptiness. Thus they may finally become open to that which can fill them.

In more traditional religious terms, it is said that sin calls forth the Savior. "Blessed fault of Adam, that gave us such a Redeemer," says the traditional chant for Easter night—blessed corruption of Adamah (which means "potter's clay" in Hebrew), whose fault was to identify himself with matter, which then enabled him to experience his nothingness.

It is from this experience of lack that the Call is born, the desire for not-being-for-death. Where could such a strange desire have come from? How could such a madness of waiting for the Unexpected have found its way into our genetic programming? What is it that transforms matter, *adamah*, a lump of clay, into Adam, the true human being capable of this essence of desire?

Meister Eckhart, a Christian whose metaphysics was very close to the Gospel of Mary, said it more simply: "If you do nothing, truly nothing, God cannot help but come into you." Unfortunately, in those who are full of themselves, there is no place for the Other. This is why he added, "If you leave, God can enter."

This means that we must leave the illusion of taking ourselves to be something, some *thing*, an object that exists in time. We must return to our true being as Subject, living in wonder at its manifestation in those transient objects that it calls its world, its body, its emotions, its personality.

When we leave behind the illusion of belief in a permanent *thing*, the Good can then come into our midst. In the heart of this finally accepted impermanence shines the presence of this unborn, unmade, uncreated "Nothing that can be found in the All of which It is the cause." This is the clear light unimpeded by the opacity of all the *things* with which we are identified. In the midst of the heavy, the light is revealed.

According to the Gospel of Mary, the Teacher came in order to help free us from the ignorance that is identification (corruption). For he is the very countenance, the incarnation, and the practice of this Good.

The Good is the manifestation of the famous triad of the ancient philosophers: goodness, truth, and beauty. The Good in this sense does not have evil as its opposite, for it means the unity of these three, the One that embraces the multiplicity of all qualities through which it is expressed.

What does goodness become when separated from light, consciousness, and truth? A softness that is the gateway to hypocrisy and compromise.

What does truth become when separated from goodness, love, and beauty? A hardness that is the gateway to fanaticism and persecution.

What does beauty become when separated from truth and goodness? Art for art's sake, an aestheticism that is the gateway to a brilliance that clarifies nothing.

Beyond the realm of opposites, the Good is the One, the doorway to Being. This Being can only manifest in a heart, body, and mind that have been emptied of all illusion, meaning all inflation and presumption; for it cannot fit into the straitjacket that they offer.

> *"This is why the Good has come into your midst.*
> *It acts together with the elements of your nature*
> *so as to reunite it with its roots."*

The radiance of Presence has come to us, and "we have seen its glory," or its *kavod*, as the Hebrews called it—the glory of the Son, "full of grace and truth," which is also that of the Father, or Source.[36]

By planting the seeds of his knowledge (the *sperma Theou*, in Greek) in the elements of our nature, the Teacher restores us to our own true heritage and ushers us back to endless resonance with our uncreated Source,

---

[36]Cf., Jn 1:14. The metaphor of Mother could just as well be used for the Source.

the "Father whom none has ever seen, and none can know,"[37] but who is revealed to us through the monogenetic Son, the Good that unites the ancient philosopher's triad. This invites us to live a life of glory, a life of love and consciousness, just as he did. This reunion with our roots is not a mere event in time, but an ever-renewed relation with the Source engendering us in every instant. It is our ignorance that creates our distance from it, and this distance involves all sorts of sickness and suffering. By an ever-new act of knowledge that is both *metanoia* (in Greek, passing beyond the known, beyond the mind and memories of which we are composed) and *teshuva* (Hebrew for the act of return, a turning about of our consciousness from our externalized, objectified being toward our inner Being), we act from the deepest heart of our lack, from the intimate space of our desire of desires. This is the space where we receive the inspiration of the Teacher and his teaching.

[Page 7, continued]
23   *Then he continued,*
24   *"This is why you become sick,*
25   *and why you die:*
26   *it is the result of your actions;*
27   *what you do takes you further away.*
28   *Those who have ears, let them hear."*

Having spoken of matter and its impermanence, and of attachment and identification with this impermanence, the Teacher now shows the consequences of ignorance and attachment.

Sickness, suffering, and death are the consequences of our acts. There is no one to blame for this, and it is vain to complain and expostulate about the evil nature of matter, the world, and humanity. There is no room here for hatred of the world, for it has been clearly stated that there is no sin, no evil. Evil and sin arise from the blamer in ourselves. It is

---

[37]None can "see" or "know" in the subject-object sense, that is.

interesting to note that in their exegesis of Revelation, some of the desert fathers of early Christianity saw the sign of deliverance in this teaching of no blame or accusation of others. "He is dead, the blamer of our brothers," they said.

This blamer is the *shatan* (or "obstacle," in Hebrew), the *diabolos* (or "divider," in Greek) in us. When he is dead, and there is no longer a place for him in us, we are free. The slave, the victim, and therefore the blamer of circumstances, is dead in us because it is no longer fed. It is replaced by the Living, symbolized as the Son who takes all responsibility for what happens. We cease to accuse others or ourselves, and instead begin to observe the pattern of causes and effects that have led to this state of sickness, suffering, and death. It is a condition that can be remedied only through a transformation of our own actions, attitudes, and ways of life. The Savior is to be found within, not elsewhere. The source of knowledge enabling us to understand what happens to us is found within. No other person can dictate to any one of us some attitude or course of action that we then must follow blindly.

The Teacher prefers us with our eyes open. He is that intelligence within us that opens our hearts and our eyes to the outside, to that world in which—either for a long time or a short time more—we must live, feel, think, hurt, cry, laugh, and love.

His teaching is liberating, but it is also demanding. If you are sick, you must stop blaming your early childhood, your parents, society, the Church, the "evil world," and so forth—and stop blaming yourself as well! This is the great teaching that recurs in the other gospels as well: "Do not judge. For your own judgment will judge you."[38]

Observe, be attentive, see what can be done; but do not waste your time, your energy, and your soul with any sort of blame. You are the result of your actions and attitudes, and it is only through them that you can be transformed and hope for a better life.

Even death—or what you imagine to be death—is the consequence of

---

[38]Cf., Mt 7:1; Lk 6:37.

your actions and attitudes. That which you call death is the expression of a disordered intellect that has long ago identified your *self* with your mortal body, along with its thoughts, emotions, and mortal attachments. As we said earlier, this disordered perception is the fruit of your corrupted nature.

> *"[W]hat you do takes you further away."*

Something important is being communicated here, and it implies a deep and transformative questioning of ourselves. Are the things we do—with regard to our work, relationships, lifestyle, attitudes—bringing us closer to Being? Or are they taking us further away? Do our actions awaken the Good in us, where truth, goodness, and beauty are One? Or are they inclining us to live more and more with bitterness, aversion, lies, ill will, and violence? Is all that we do bringing us closer to the Son within us, to intimacy with his and our Origin in the breath of the Spirit? Or does it take us further away, toward exile from our true identity, so that we become slaves to circumstances—whether favorable or unfavorable—and thereby cut ourselves off from our true Life and Source, which in every instant give us our being?

In sum, are my actions the expression of Being, or are they a caricature of it? Are they a manifestation of it, or a repression of it?

> *Do my acts express my word?*
> *Does my word express my thought?*
> *Does my thought express my desire?*
> *Does my desire express my being?*
> *Does my being express the Being That Is What It Is (YHWH),*
> *   the I AM that calls me to be?*

This is not some mundane examination of conscience. It is conscience (or consciousness) itself, the consciousness of myself as a path—either a path of return, or a path that goes further and further away.

It can be an act of presence in which everything becomes strangely present regardless of whether the content is agreeable or disagreeable, for this is the very presence of the Being that constantly creates all being.

But it can also become an act of absence in which everything becomes strangely absent, a wasteland of missing Being. In this mode everything, however stimulating or entertaining, has the stale taste of exile deep down. Whether the content is agreeable or disagreeable is of no real importance because everything ultimately feels empty of meaning. This is the path that can take you far away from home, sometimes indulging a belief that no return is possible, that *home* does not exist, and that meaninglessness and absurdity are inherent in the human condition.

The choice here is mine alone: How shall I use my intelligence and my imagination?

The Teacher himself made it clear: Your unhappiness is the consequence of your actions, and your actions are the consequence of your choice—what you do takes you further away. As Paul of Tarsus put it: "Instead of the good you desire, you do the evil you do not desire."[39]

"Those who have ears let them hear."

Nothing and no one can compel those who do not wish to understand. Once more, the Teacher confronts us unsentimentally—yet in fathomless love—with our own freedom. It is not we who make the path; it is we who give it direction. This is our true power: We direct our path right into the heart of sickness and suffering, toward the Good.

Perhaps the world has no meaning in itself—it is given to us to discover one. This of course requires courage. But more than anything else, it requires imagination—that sublime imagination that may be glimpsed in certain thoughts hastily dismissed as crazy by those who ignore them, or heard in certain poems, in certain angelic messages . . . and in all of the great sacred texts.

[39]Rom 7:19.

[Page 8]

1   "Attachment to matter
2   gives rise to passion against nature.
3   Thus trouble arises in the whole body;
4   this is why I tell you:
5   'Be in harmony . . .'
6   If you are out of balance,
7   take inspiration from manifestations
8   of your true nature.
9   Those who have ears,
10   let them hear."

Ignorance, a sickness of the heart and the mind, is accompanied by attachment, which is a sickness of desire. It is at once a blockage of true desire, and an inflation of emotional desire—a fixation upon some object in which desire imagines it will find fulfillment and repose.

The Teacher speaks here of attachment to matter. If we take this to mean all that is composed, and that will someday be decomposed, then he is not just talking about attachment to our house in the country or our stock portfolio. He also means attachment to a person or people, to a country or society, or to anything that we make into an *object* belonging to us. This is what Yeshua is speaking of in other gospels, when, for example, he warns against looking upon a woman with lust. For with this look a man does not see the woman herself, but a mere object of possible pleasure. It misses the subject that she is, as well as any true relation—infinitely richer than that of possession—that might be established with her.

Our ideologies and beliefs are also subtle forms of matter in this sense, for they are composed of images and concepts. Attachment to these may be far stronger than to people or to objects of lust and may take us further away from our freedom, making us dependent and generating the "passion against nature" spoken of in these lines.

It is important to note that nowhere is it implied that matter, people, or objects are bad or harmful in themselves. It is our attachments and our passions[40] that are against nature. For the Teacher, it would seem that it is not our true nature to attach ourselves to that which we know to be transitory and impermanent. It is natural, in this sense, to love beings and things for what they are: a "radiant dew," as the prophet Isaiah said—one that can reflect the rising sun, and bring us great joy. But attachment and the desire to perpetuate that which was not made to last can be seen in this light to show simple stupidity, if not insanity.

"Thus trouble arises in the whole body." Even before we take the trouble to think about it, our body already knows quite well that its cherished treasures will be taken away. When a physician tries to reassure a dying patient with false optimism, trouble arises—the doctor's attempts creates a kind of schizophrenic double bind that can engender more suffering than before. The body knows very well what its ultimate destiny is, and a person in this situation is in need of a different kind of word, addressed to something other than that which is ultimately destined to be decomposed.

The Teacher never preaches any sort of belief system. Instead, he reminds us of facts that are both hard to hear and good to hear: Attachment and passion against nature only add soul-troubles to our body-troubles. His aim is for us to abandon this state so as to return to our true nature. As Saint John of Damascus, an early Christian father, phrased it: "Conversion is the return to what is with nature from what is against it."

To look at an object, a person, or a landscape with love and without attachment, with no desire for appropriation of it, is to see it more clearly. This clear seeing also allows the gift to appear, revealed to us through the object, person, or scene. Nothing is owed to us, everything is given to us. We were not created to possess, but to "be with . . . " This has implications that challenge all our usual notions of responsibility, for these ideas are generally developed within the context of our notions of ownership.

To think that we can really possess any object or person—even our own bodies, our own thoughts, or our own lives—is an illusion. This illusion is

---

[40]Latin *passio*, from Greek *pathos*, "suffering"; also the root of our word *pathology*.

the cause of trouble, the fundamental insecurity that undermines our greatest riches, our dearest loves, our highest thoughts, and our deepest devotions. Because it sets up a relationship of power and dependence, it is the opposite of true relationship, which is in harmony with all that is:

> *this is why I tell you:*
> *'Be in harmony . . .'*

To be in harmony is to be in a conscious and loving relationship with what is. Here, there is no willing or desiring of particulars, for that would imply a fixation on an illusory separate part of the flowing totality in which we live. Harmony means to have a musical relationship with the world, to enter into resonance, to be in tune with all that is.

To enter into resonance with the world is a long work of attuning that demands a quality of listening—an all-embracing, extraordinary attention to being. Is it others, and the world, who should attune to us (as we are so often in the habit of demanding)? Or is it we ourselves who should attune to them?

The Teacher seems to be telling us that it is indeed our task to enter into resonance with whatever environment we find ourselves in, and even to tune into our adversary, before it is too late:

> *If you go to the altar to make an offering, and remember*
> *something that your brother holds against you,*
> *set aside your offering, go first to be reconciled with your*
> *brother, and then go make your offering.*
> *Act quickly to be in accord with your adversary, while you are*
> *still on the way with him."* [41]

And of course he goes even further than this when he tells his disciples to love their enemies, to tune into them so as to "be perfect, just as

---

[41]Mt 5:23–25.

your heavenly Father is perfect,"[42] or "merciful, just as your Father is merciful."[43]

But how are we to be in harmony with our enemies? And how do we attune ourselves to forces that want to harm or destroy us? Certainly this is not a teaching that is telling us to simply give in to these forces and let them have their way. Such adversaries must be confronted in all their violence—but without adding to it, without provoking new violence. To "be in harmony" with our enemies is to skillfully allow their violence to pass through us without contaminating us. Just as in the martial arts, this attunement to our attackers can then awaken a consciousness in them that could help them to get out of the trouble they are in.

"An eye for an eye, a tooth for a tooth"—those who abide by this old principle have not yet attained the higher law of harmony. But still less is it attained through escapism or cowardice—"To him who strikes you on one cheek, offer the other one also." These words are often misunderstood. It is important to note that it is not the *same* cheek that is being offered again—that would indeed suggest some form of masochism or morbid acquiescence. Offering the *other* cheek means presenting an entirely new and unexpected way of dealing with the problem. It means to oppose violence with consciousness, to look the other in the eye, to regard the other as subject like oneself, and to refuse to be a predictable object. To be in harmony is to enter into resonance with other subjects, with other liberties. But this cannot happen without friction and conflict. Is it even possible?

Certainly it is easier for violins than for human beings to be attuned to each other. This is at least partly because we are "out of balance," as the Teacher says. Before trying to harmonize with the world and with others, it is surely necessary to be in harmony with yourself. How can an instrument that is out of tune with itself be tuned to other instruments,

---

[42]Mt 5:43–48.

[43]Lk 6:27, 28, 32–36. It is interesting to note that while Matthew speaks of perfection, Luke speaks of mercy. What did Yeshua say? Neither one, to be sure, or both together! For what is perfection without mercy or mercy without perfection?

regardless of whether or not they also need tuning? To care for one's instrument, to harmonize head, heart, and body, is the first condition for any possibility of harmony with others. If people have no inner peace, how are they to find it outside of themselves? If the different quarters of our inner Jerusalem are not united, how can we possibly accomplish this in the outer Jerusalem? In each of these quarters there is a cult that claims superiority over the whole city. In human beings, it may be emotion, reason, or instinct that becomes such an inner cult, attempting to dominate the entire composite human. Yet this composite was created for harmony, for a communion in which each part is there to serve the others.

Harmony may manifest when oppositions suddenly discover themselves to be quite complementary, so that discordances themselves are integrated into a higher order of harmony where it is at last recognized that each is contributing to the symphony of the All.

When your instrument is out of tune, when you are surrounded by discordance, and you find yourself in disharmony (perhaps to the extremes of fear, contempt, hatred), then "take inspiration from manifestations of your true nature," or, as it might also be translated, from images of your true nature—but in the imaginal, not the imaginary, sense of the word.

When you are out of balance, simply acknowledge it instead of indulging in it—or worse, justifying or blaming yourself.[44] Allow yourself to be inspired by manifestations of the fully human and incarnations of the peace and harmony that we know is possible in ourselves.

In this particular context of Yeshua as divine manifestation within the human, Paul of Tarsus described the Teacher as "the Image of the invisible God."[45] To take inspiration from such an image is more than just receiving positive feelings from an icon, for this icon is a window into the invisible, where we see what humanness is capable of, where we see the incarnation of love that is our true calling. As John the Evangelist said, "If

---

[44]Or comparing yourself favorably with those who are even more unbalanced: "In the land of the blind, the one-eyed is king."

[45]Col 1:15. As manifestation of wisdom, Yeshua is the reflection of God (Wisdom 7:26) prior to all creatures (Prv 8:27–30), who leads human beings to God (Prv 8:31–36).

Yeshua had not come, there would be no sin." In other words, if we had never been able to know of an authentic human being, we would be ignorant of the fact that we are not yet human. If we had never seen a human in true health, we would not know that we are sick. If we had never seen a truly balanced human, whose desire is properly oriented, we would not know of the disorientation of our own desire.

> *"If you are out of balance,*
> *take inspiration from manifestations*
> *of your true nature."*

In fact, this is an exercise advocated by all the great spiritual traditions. It is essential for anyone who would truly engage in a spiritual path, yet it may take different forms, such as spending time in the company of wise and holy people or visiting special places where their presence is felt; and taking inspiration from the actions and attitudes of those beings who incarnate our own true nature and manifest what is both completely human and fully divine in us—those whose inner truth, beauty, and goodness are the signs of the forgotten God who dwells within us.

This passage concludes with the Teacher's recurrent phrase reminding us that these signs are especially for those who dwell in wholehearted attention and thus know how to look and listen deeply to slow and subtle gestures:

> *"Those who have ears,*
> *let them hear."*

[Page 8, continued]
11   *After saying this, the Blessed One*
12   *greeted them all, saying:*
13   *"Peace be with you — may my Peace*
14   *arise and be fulfilled within you!"*

Note that this is the only passage where this gospel refers to the Teacher Yeshua as the "Blessed One"—the embodiment of bliss.

This is a good place to pause and consider the following propositions:

> Pleasure is the delight and fulfillment of the body *(soma)*.
> Happiness is the delight and fulfillment of the soul (psyche).
> Joy is the delight and fulfillment of the spirit (nous).

All of these delights and fulfillments are the reverberations within a created being of uncreated Bliss, a more or less limited participation in the Being of the Blessed One. In this sense, all pleasure, happiness, and joy are relative, yet they are also sacred.

Bliss is the delight and fulfillment of the Holy Spirit (Pneuma) in humankind, and it is this blessing that the Teacher embodies. He engenders pleasure, happiness, and joy through reflections of the light of the blessing that fills him. When his peace and equanimity arise and are fulfilled within us, these are the closest, most intimate reflections of the secrets of his quickening life.

Though the Teacher emphasizes the trouble *(tarakhe)* that arises from our ignorance, he emphasizes even more the arising of his peace.

> *"Peace be with you—may my Peace*
> *arise and be fulfilled within you!"*

The preceeding pages show that this peace is first of all *eukrasia* (harmony, literally "good mixture," "good proportions"), or, more precisely, balance. The injunction to "be in harmony" could also be translated as to "be well-balanced" *(soōpe etetnētnhēt)*. This invites the disciples to be *eukratoï*, those who are balanced and at peace in body, soul, and spirit.

This experience of *krasis* (mingling or mixing) is dealt with in the Hippocratic medical tradition. It explains all bodily and psychic suffering as a lack of harmony *(anarmostein)* among the composite elements of the human being. But the peace offered by the Teacher goes even further than a state of harmony, balance, or wholeness (*shalom* in Hebrew also refers to this state, for to wish someone *shalom* is to wish them to dwell in wholeness). The peace of the Teacher is his very Presence, and is none other than permanent contact with the divine and joyous Source of breath itself.

This peace is the Father who in Spirit engenders the Son in us. It is not a physical or a psychic peace, for either one of these is always more or less dependent on favorable circumstances. Instead, it is an unconditional peace that no one and nothing can take from us (Jn 14:27):

> *"I leave you my peace,*
> *I give you my peace,*
> *I do not give it to you as the world gives it."*

The world offers pacifiers, reassurances, euphoria; it does not offer "the peace which never passes," for this peace is the Other. It is the I AM, the presence of Being that remains through whatever good or bad times are being lived.

At this point it is useful to recall the parallels between the Gospel of Mary and the canonical Gospels, based on the work of Anne Pasquier.[46] [Note: Italics in the following chart are Leloup's.—*Trans.*]

GOSPEL OF MARY	NEW TESTAMENT
"Peace be with you" (Mary 8:13).	"Peace be with you" (Lk 24:36; Jn 20:19, 21, 26). (During the first appearances of Jesus after his resurrection.)
"May *my peace* arise . . . within you" (Mary 8:13–14).	"Peace I leave with you. It is *my peace* that I give you" (Jn 14:27). (During the Savior's farewells after the Last Supper, announcing his journey to the Father and the coming of

---

[46]Pasquier, *L'Evangile de Marie,* 57–58. See also W. C. Till and H. M. Schenke, *Die gnostischen Schriften,* 64–65, and R. Mcl. Wilson, "The New Testament in the Gnostic Gospel of Mary," in Robinson, *The Nag Hammadi Library,* 242–43.

	the Holy Spirit; various sayings regarding signs and the coming of the Son of Man, cf. Mk 13:5; Lk 21:8.)
"Be vigilant, and allow no one to mislead you" (Mary 8:15–16).	*"Take care that none deceive you* for many will come in my name saying 'I am the Christ'" (Mt 24:4–5).
" . . . by saying 'Here it is!' or 'There it is!' " (Mary 8:16–18).	"Therefore, if anyone tells you, 'Look, here is the Christ,' or 'There he is,' do not believe them" (Mt 24:23. Cf. Mk 13:5; Lk 21:8).
	"Men will tell you 'Here it is,' or 'There it is'" (Lk 17:23). On the presence of the Kingdom: "When the Pharisees asked him when the Kingdom of God would come, he replied, 'The Kingdom of God does not come with your careful observation, nor will people say *Here it is, or there it is . . .*'" (Lk 17:20–21).
"For it is within you that the Son of Man dwells" (Mary 8:19–20).	" . . . for the Kingdom of God *is within you*" (ιδοὺ γὰρ ἡ βασιλεία τοῦ θεοῦ ἐντὸζ ὑμῶν ἐστιν, Lk 17:21).
"Go to him" (Mary 8:21).	"If anyone would come after me, he must deny himself and take up his cross and follow me" (Mt 16:24; cf Mk 8:34; Lk 9:23). (After the first announcement of the Passion.)
"For those who seek him, find him" (Mary 8:22).	"Seek and ye shall find" (Mt 7:7; cf Lk 11:9). (Seeking the Kingdom and the treasure of Heaven.)
"Walk forth, and announce the *gospel of the Kingdom*" (Mary 8:23–24).	"And this *gospel of the Kingdom* will be preached in the whole world as a testimony to all nations, and then the end will come" (Mt 24:24; cf. Mk 13:10). (Of signs and the coming of the Son of Man.) "Go unto all the world and preach the gospel to all creation" (Mk 16:15).

"Impose no law other than that which I have witnessed. Do not add more laws to those given in the Torah, lest you become bound by them" (Mary 9:1–4).

"But now, by dying to *what once bound us,* we have been released from the law . . . " (νυνὶ δὲ κατηργήθημεν ἀπὸ του νόμου, ἀποθανόντες ἓι ψ κατείχόμεθα, Rom 7:6).

This peace that the Teacher offers us is a seed. After it has taken root in good soil, it still must grow.[47] We are not yet in peace, for this peace is a process of becoming, a work that we accomplish—or rather that we *allow* to be accomplished—within us. Nowhere else will it be found, and no one can sell or rent it to us. There may well appear merchants of happiness with pacifiers that can calm the troubles of our days and nights for a while. But there are no merchants of beatitude. There is only a Presence that is to be discovered, and allowed to grow, in the very core of ourselves.

This recalls the story of the woman who was looking for her lost jewels in the village square.[48] The other villagers wished her well, and were trying to help her find this treasure in the area in and around the square. They had been searching fruitlessly for some time, when someone asked her: "But exactly where did you lose this treasure?"

"I lost it in my home," the woman answered

"But are you crazy? If you lost it in your home, why are you having us help you search out here in the square?"

"And you, my friend," she replied, "is this not what you are always doing, searching for your treasure in the streets, in the square, when it is really in your own home that you lost what you most want? Don't you go everywhere in vain search of peace and happiness, your greatest treasure, which you have lost in your own home? In your own heart—that is where you must search. It is there that your treasure has always been waiting to be found."

---

[47] See the parables of the sowing of the seeds: Mt 13:3; Mk 4:3; Lk 8:9.
[48] [An ancient story, versions of which are found in many oral traditions.—*Trans.*]

Yet another version[49] of this story tells of a man searching for his lost key out in the street underneath the lamp, because the light is better there than in his house.

Many search for peace where there seems to be the most light—the light of explanations, reasons, and justifications; the relative light of our small worlds and our supposed knowledge. But the abode of peace is not to be found there. Sometimes we must venture into the darkest rooms of our house and search in certain corners of the unconscious. There is darkness that turn out to be more brilliant than our little lamps and fireflies. In the night, stars may be revealed, and they may bring the mysterious light of peace far more than the brightest neon can do.

[Page 8, continued]

15   *"Be vigilant, and allow no one to mislead you*

16   *by saying:*

17   *'Here it is!' or*

18   *'There it is!'*

19   *For it is within you*

20   *that the Son of Man dwells.*

21   *Go to him,*

22   *for those who seek him, find him."*

Today, as in the time of Yeshua, messiahs abound. Their promises still sell well, and there are plenty of people ready to leave everything to follow them. The followers' disillusionment is often immense, as is the suffering that ensues, which sometimes includes fatalities.

The Teacher's warning in verses 15 through 22 is as relevant as ever. "Here it is! There it is!"—this warning against messianic pretensions could refer primarily to a person, whether a man or a woman, but it always implies a person who offers to take away our burdens, solve our problems, heal or at least bandage all our wounds, and especially, think our thoughts

---

[49]Well known in the Middle East, the story of the Sufi fool-sage Mullah Nasruddin.

for us. It may also refer to a messianic ideology or movement, a magical panacea, or even a form of legislation or state decree that promises to restore everything to order.

On the other hand, there are phenomena that seem to fall in this general category yet demand special consideration, such as the numerous appearances of the Virgin, which often attract huge crowds. It seems that our history of repression of the Feminine is still unable to prevent it from breaking through in such manifestations—often during times and contexts where it is most repressed.

Interestingly, the messages of these apparitions have been quite clear for the most part: Do not become attached to their forms, but repent and return to yourself through means such as prayer or fasting; rediscover the experience of *being* rather than *doing* and accumulating things; and renew in yourself the art of giving and receiving rather than producing and exploiting. Our purpose on Earth is not to manipulate things, these messages tell us, but to meet each other in living encounters. Life is too short to be lived by exploiting each other. There is something better for us to do, and the time we have is barely enough to learn how to love one another.

And no one can learn this for us, because no matter how we may search outside ourselves for he or she who will save us from the burden of our freedom, no matter where we travel in our searching, if the message we find is authentic, it will send us right back to ourselves, "For it is within you *(entōs humōn)* that the Son of Man dwells."[50]

It is important to note that the teachings of the apparitions, the canonical Gospels, and the Gospel of Mary Magdalene all agree on this point. As long as our peace is dependent on any kind of external reality, it is not Peace; as long as our love for others and for the world is dependent on attitudes and feelings toward us, it is not Love. To the extent that our life depends on the material circumstances and conditions that constitute us, it is not yet Life. It is still within the domain of the *outer person,* who

---

[50]Lk 17:21 and the Gospel of Thomas 3. On the theme of the Kingdom within and its parallels, see Puech, *En quête de gnose,* vol. 2 (Paris: Gallimard), 270–79.

is destined to fall in ruins. It is still within a universe that is subject to the laws of entropy and daily decay.

Only within our true being do we find a Reality, a Life, a Knowledge, a Love, and a Peace that are not dependent. These are the Son of Man, who is also the Son of God.

This Reality is both who we are, and what we must become.

❧

On Friday, October 29, 1943, in the midst of the Nazi horror that had overtaken Hungary, a voice spoke to Gitta Mallasz and her friends:

> *The created world, and the creative world.*
> *Between the two: the Abyss.*
> *Be sure you understand this!*
> *You yourself are the bridge.*
> *It will not avail you to desire the radiance of creation,*
> *When you, within yourself, are the bridge.*
> *This has been given to you.*[51]

The correspondence between the vision the words of this voice conjure and that of the Son of Man, which we are and yet must become, is worth exploring a bit further. Years later, in conversation with her friend Patrice Van Eersel, Gitta Mallasz drew a figure representing four levels of reality (see figure 1)—we might be tempted to use the word *theanthropos* (*theos* meaning "God," *anthropos* meaning "human") for the subject of the diagram, if it were not a bit heavy and pedantic. In any case, as we see, the human being—the incomplete human—is at the center of a figure that can be seen as a bridge between created and creative (divine) realms.

Note the dotted lines in the center of the diagram. "Completion consists of transforming the dotted lines into a continuous curve joining with the other levels in such a way as to suggest a sudden metamorphosis into

---

[51]Gitta Mallasz, *Dialogue avec l'ange* (Aubier, 1996). For a complete English translation, see Gitta Mallasz, *Talking with Angels* (Continuum Books, 1998).

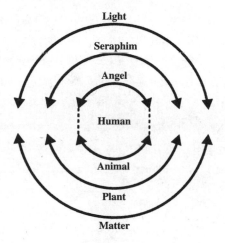

Figure 1

a single, vast and inconceivable universal consciousness," says Patrice Van Eersel, in his own spirited interpretation of the diagram (see figure 2.)[52]

While preserving the basic vision of the illustration, I wish to add some further categories, using somewhat different terms (see figure 3). But the message remains essentially the same and may help us to understand the

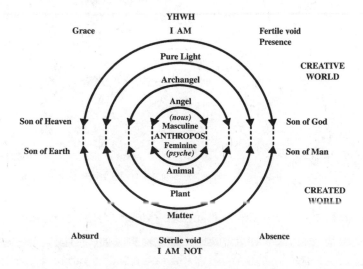

Figure 2

[52]Patrice Van Eersel, *La source blanche* (Paris: Grasset, 1996).

possibility of the birth in us of the authentic human, which is none other than the *theandros*, the divine-human, as Soloviev says.[53]

We know that humanity is a bridge. It must form the link between the two shores of the created and the creative worlds, the sons of heaven and of earth, the Son of Man and the Son of God. Some well-known Gnostic doctrines prefer to speak in terms of *androgyne* —the union of the masculine and feminine principles, but my preference shall be to follow the Gospel of Mary, and use the term *anthropos* (see figure 3).

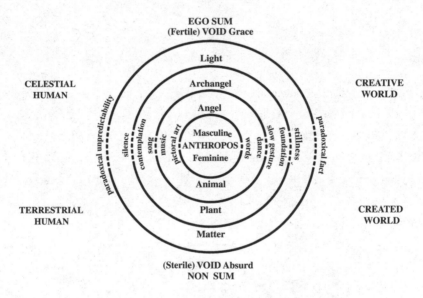

Figure 3

This pattern, with ANTHROPOS at the center, recalls the structure of the brain, with its two hemispheres and their opposite or complementary functions. The corpus callosum, which unites the two halves of the brain, is thus analogous to humanness, in both its fragility and its greatness. The full potential for union of these opposites, Eastern and Western, intuitive and logical, diurnal and nocturnal, is rarely realized, either on the cosmological or the neurological level.

---

[53]Soloviev, *Leçons sur la théandricité* (St. Petersburg, 1957); and *A Solviev Anthology*, 2001.

Let us note that we are the bridge between *animal* and *angel* primarily through the faculty of language, whether in thought or imagination, whether expressed or unexpressed. The link here is the word, or the expression of desire, beyond mere need and demand. Human beings become the bridge between *plant* and *archangel* in the heart, through the slow gesture—movement that is both supple and permeated with awareness.

We are the bridge between *I AM* and *I am not*, between the *fertile void* and the *sterile void*, through the experience that is both foreseen and unforseeable, such as the sudden appearance of a rainbow in a storm at noon. The sterile void, with its stagnant absurdity, is what Nicolai Berdyaev called the "bad nothingness." To become a bridge between it and the fertile void, the uncreated Origin of all being, is to embrace and live in one instant both the absurdity and the grace of the human condition.

"To be *or* not to be" is not at all the question, for it is revealed as an expression of torment and even stupidity. To be *and* not to be—that is the question! This restores us to harmony both with ancient esoteric teaching and the implications of quantum physics.

Of course the description, analysis, and especially the building, of these different bridges will demand from us more extensive development. But it is when we become bridges ourselves that we have the possibility to be both fully human and fully divine, in the image and the likeness of that which the ancients called the "archetype of synthesis."

Meanwhile, the Gospel of Mary tells us to "Go to him" (Mary 8:21), to verify each of his teachings for ourselves, and to become what he is so as to discover what we eternally are.

The next verse says that "they who seek him, find him."[54] For the Savior is this desire that makes us seek him, the dotted line that is ours to fill in. And then we can marvel at the splendor of his—and our—visage. In truth, we would not be seeking him, if we had not already found him.

---

[54]Cf. Mt 7:8, Lk 11:10, and the Gospel of Thomas 2 and 92.

[Page 8, continued]

23   *"Walk forth,*

24   *and announce the gospel of the Kingdom."*[55]

Human beings are on a road. As with health, happiness is surely also found in walking. Suffering or disease (*mahala* in Hebrew) comes from our being arrested in such a way that we turn in circles inside the prisons of body, thought, and soul that are called pain, ignorance, and madness. When the great myths present the ways of healing as paths or experiences full of pain, we should consider this as only a stage, a pause during which the mind is temporarily bound to reflection. But this can be neither home nor harbor for the wayfaring soul of the true walker.

The ways are many, yet the Way is one. There are ways by sea, ways by land, storms and shipwrecks, buried treasures and promised lands. There are exiles and returns, Icarus-like ascents and falls, yet there are also heavenly journeys and the Assumption, which are without return. There are ways of fire where the voyager is consumed, or reborn from ashes like the phoenix, relying on the lightning flashes of the night for illumination.

All of these are metaphors to be contemplated, as well as adventures to be lived. Our goal is to keep going beyond that which confines and imprisons—yet which can never contain us—toward a sublime opening of the psyche or soul, which in the very act of accepting its limits, connects with a dimension that death cannot define.

This is why the Teacher keeps telling those whom he encounters on the way: "Walk forth!"

Recent scholarship has found that previous translations of the eight beatitudes in the Gospel of Matthew are in error inasmuch as they imply a kind of passive consolation in the face of tribulations. They are instead an invitation to stand up, to arise and walk forth, no matter what pain and trouble may lie on the road ahead. When we return to the original Semitic terms underlying the Greek version of Jesus' words in this gospel,

---

[55]See Mt 4:23 and 9:35; Lk 4:43 and 81; Acts 8:12.

we find that *blessed* should be replaced by *walk forth*, which restores the text's original dynamic quality.[56]

Walk forth, you in whom the breath (spirit) is held back and restrained by emotions and by fear!

Walk forth, you gentle and humble ones, for your gentleness is your strength. The earth resists those who are violent, and offers herself to those who respect her. As the Indian proverb says, "Walk softly upon the earth, for she is sacred." To act more gently is not to act more feebly or slowly, it is to act with more consciousness and love. Now we begin to understand why the earth is given as the rightful heritage of the gentle, and denied to the violent.

Walk forth, you who weep, for you shall be consoled! Chouraqui translates *you who weep* as *those who mourn*. To mourn authentically is to accept that what is past is past, an indispensable condition for going further. This does not mean we should refrain from tears or other emotions, but that we are not to indulge in them. It means to pass through them, walking forth toward a higher serenity and more sensitive maturity.

Walk forth, those who starve and thirst for justice! Yes, they shall be satisfied! Thus those who hunger and thirst must not remain static, for they are on a quest; and the quest for justice, which is also holiness, can never be final. Yet this does not imply some perpetual dissatisfaction, but

---

[56][See André Chouraqui, trans., *La Bible* (Desclée de Brouwer, 1989) for a renowned translation of these famous words of Jesus in Mt 5, known as the Beatitudes. Chouraqui's translation of the Bible is an important reference in France because it makes minimal concession to literary readability so as to stay very close to the original, literal sense of the Hebrew (OT) and Greek (NT), while also making use of Aramaic and Syriac sources. Sometimes his translations are strikingly different from all familiar ones. An example is the phrase normally rendered as "Blessed are . . . ," which begins each of the beatitudes in all conventional translations. Chouraqui renders this as "En marche!" (or "Walk forth!"). This is a radical departure from the usual translation not only in meaning, but also in mood, which in "Walk forth!" becomes imperative—in other words, a command to action. The words usually translated as "poor in spirit" are also rendered with radical literalism, so that the first beatitude now begins as: "Walk forth, the humiliated of breath!" ("En marche, les humiliés du souffle!") As in Greek, the word for *spirit* in Semitic langauages derives from that for *breath*.

Other passages from Mt 5 given in quotation marks in the text above are our literal English translations of Chouraqui's French. He almost always prefers to use the Hebrew word *Elohim* instead of *God*. Leloup's paraphrases of Chouraqui are given without quotation marks.—*Trans.*]

the knowledge that the perfectibility of humanity and of the world is infinite, an undertaking that can have no final conclusion.

Walk forth, the pure of heart! Yes, you shall see Elohim! To see the Other, our vision must be emptied of presuppositions and judgments. Hence in order to see God, it is even more imperative that we embark on a long walk—one of distancing ourselves from our projections—even the most seductively beautiful—that we often take for spiritual experiences, even for an experience of God. But these have nothing to do with the divine Reality, for they are still much too bound up with our ego and its infantile dreams of omnipotence. We may know the attributes and qualities of Being, but only the pure of heart can taste Being as it is, without qualities and in its true holiness, which is beyond all comparison.

Walk forth, merciful ones! You shall receive mercy![57] Happy are those who are able to remain sensitive to the misery and suffering of others. The future belongs to the pure and gentle, not to the rigid purists of all our fundamentalism. If the latter have the purity of angels, they also have the pride of demons, like all grand and petty inquisitors who shed blood in the name of purity, religious faith, traditional values, or race. The greatest crimes against humanity are always committed in the name of goodness and the need to preserve integrity and purity. We have yet to fully appreciate the danger and delusion of purity without mercy.

The pure of heart and the merciful are commanded to walk forth, because we can never have too much compassion for the challenge of understanding the suffering and misery of another. And we can never have a heart too pure and sensitive for the challenge of seeing another's true potential, for both forgiving everything and demanding everything of another. "To understand all is to forgive all," as Plato said long ago. "The more I know, the more I love; the more I love, the more I know," said

---

[57][In this passage Chouraqui uses the word *matriciels*, whereas Leloup uses the customary *misericordieux* (merciful). *Matriciel* is strange enough in French, and has no exact English equivalent, but the image is that of the womb, of being endowed with a womblike or maternal quality. The intent is to preserve the image conveyed in Semitic languages, where *womb* is the etymological root of all words for "compassion," "mercy," and so forth.—*Trans.*]

Saint Catherine of Sienna a millennium later. The more truly pure of heart I am, the more my heart sees, and the more merciful it is. And the more merciful it is, the more it sees, and the purer it becomes.

Walk forth, peacemakers! Yes, you shall be acclaimed sons of Elohim! Peace is the fruit of an artisan's work. It is the slowest and most patient way of walking. Peace cannot be commanded by throwing money at a problem, nor by overthrowing a government. It is nothing less than the Son of Man and the Son of God being born within ourselves.

Yeshua's earthly father was an artisan who taught him how to plane and polish the most difficult woods. This is not unrelated to the patience and love that the Teacher needed in order to plane and polish souls so that they can reveal their beauty, thereby adapting better to other souls and fulfilling their true service.

Walk forth, those persecuted for justice's sake! Yes, the kingdom of heaven is theirs!

Walk forth, when they insult and persecute you, accusing you of all sorts of crimes because of me. Be in joy and lightness, because your reward is great in heaven. Indeed, this is how the prophets who came before you were persecuted.

Yeshua is not saying "Blessed are you, unhappy victims, be happy in your martyrdom." He is saying "Do not let yourself be stopped by persecution, slander, and all sorts of violence. Use these as a challenge and opportunity for growing in consciousness and in love. Discover within yourself the same patience (passion) that I found when faced by my adversaries. This is truly your opportunity to live the greatest of exercises, which is love of one's enemies." You will then discover within yourself that "terrifying force of humble love," which is able to "forgive them, for they know not what they do." Thus you continue to teach your enemies not only with your words, but with your acts.

Walk forth, and announce the gospel of the Kingdom. It is through the very power and simplicity of your becoming that you announce the Kingdom that is to come. You bear witness that it is possible to live in surrender to another kind of consciousness and a different mind, and that a new being lives within you. You will live no more in the thrall of the empire of your past, your unconscious, or your social surroundings. Your acts will be determined by the most intimate part of your being, that place where nothing is forced, where it is Spirit that inspires you—that Spirit of whom "none can say whence It cometh, nor where It goeth" (Jn 3:8), though ontologically (in the language of Yeshua and Mary's time) it comes from the Father and returns to the Father. It is the conscious Breath that comes from the unnamable space where inspiration originates, and expiration returns—that space without boundaries, which we are sometimes fortunate enough to taste when silence reigns within us.

Walk forth, and announce the good news of knowledge and teachings that will be needed for this transformation in which human beings can finally begin to become fully human. Keep on walking on this road, where you become both more human and more divine. May each day bring you a little less under the sway of the fears, inhibitions, and lies that are certainly the heritage of your individual and collective past, yet in which (consciously or unconsciously) you still indulge in the present. And may each day bring you more and more surrender to freedom and love. For these are fruits of your most beautiful dreams and of the purest desire that—consciously or unconsciously, but consciously above all, so as to savor it fully—you can ever experience in the present.

[Page 9]

1. *"Impose no law*
2   *other than that which I have witnessed.*
3   *Do not add more laws to those given in the Torah,*
4   *lest you become bound by them."*

Michel Tardieu offers the following with regard to this warning about rules or laws *(horos):*

There is no *horos* other than that of the "gospel of the Kingdom" implied in the previous passage—and that is not a written *horos*. This is a rhetoric directed against the ecclesiastical decree of a canon of only four legitimate gospels.[58] The gospel of the Kingdom is declared as the only new law, thus opposing any attempts to imitate the lawgiver, i.e., Moses, considered to be the author of the Torah by Church authority.

Here we have an echo of the resistance of certain early Christian circles to the ecclesiastical decision to limit the canon of its own scriptures (the New Testament) and to recognize the Jewish Bible as the Old Testament.

The invocation of the Kingdom implies an inward kind of rule, a gospel that arises from inner revelation and not from some outer authority's decision (law, testament). . . . [59]

These reflections of an eminent Dominican scholar pose no problem for us so far. But we cannot accept his subsequent interpretation of this passage as an example of anti-Semitism—or more precisely, an anti-Judaism that would be even more radical than that which already exists in the New Testament,[60] and as a polemic against the decision of ecclesiastical authority to honor the Torah along with its own scriptures. Tardieu claims that this passage of the Gospel of Mary would make it impossible for the flock [sic] to obey the Mosaic law.

Is this sort of interpretation really necessary? Does it not simply add to the multitude of misunderstandings that have set Christians against Jews ever since the time of Paul of Tarsus?[61] Yeshua clearly said: "Do not think that I have come to abolish the law or the prophets. I have not come to abolish them, but to fulfill them."[62] And he even declares that the Torah be respected in its smallest details.

---

[58][Of course, this interpretation would imply a date much beyond the lifetimes of Jesus or Mary for the writing of this passage. More literal (English) translations of this passage are somewhat different: "Do not lay down any rules beyond what I have shown you, and do not give a law like the lawgiver, lest you be constrained by it.—*Trans.*]

[59]Tardieu, *Codex de Berlin*, 229.

[60]See Jn 7:19: "Has not Moses given you the law? Yet not one of you keeps the law! Why are you trying to kill me?" For more explicit anti-Semitism, see 1 Thes 2:14–16.

[61]"Those who belong to Christ are no longer subject to the law." See Gal 5:22–25.

[62]Mt 5:17.

This is what compels us to stick to the simple and literal meaning of this text: You are not to add more laws to those already given by the law-giver, i.e., the author of the Torah.

Saint Francis of Assisi, when asked by his brothers to lay down laws for them, answered: "Do not add anything to the gospel, for we have no other rule than the gospel. Do not add to it, do not make other rules. Your rule is the gospel and he who incarnates it. Follow him, walk with him." And Saint Ignatius of Antioch said: "My law archives are simply the Christ."

The Law is not just a collection of precepts and commandments, it is an incarnation and a way of living.

> *"Impose no law*
> *other than that which I have witnessed."*

This law is that of love and freedom, of which Yeshua is the act and the flesh, and which he has witnessed with his words, his deeds, his patience, and his forgiveness.

"Be yourselves also the witnesses of love in flesh and bone; even more, be incarnations of him," said Elizabeth of the Trinity. Be creative subjects who speak and love in the midst of "inanimate" objects, thus rendering unto them their true names and souls.

"Love one another as I have loved you" (Jn 15:12). There is no other law. The problem is to live this; to become the witnessing lived by the Teacher; to love family, friends, enemies, men and women *as* he loved them; to love the Source of all that lives and breathes, as he did. The *as* in this verse from John is not the *as* of comparison. It does not invite us to imitate, which would only result in caricature. Rather, it is telling us to allow this law of life to be—it is already within us, like the sap that runs in the tree, helping it to hold firm as well as to bend to the winds.

The Teacher is not some external image that we should try to resemble. He is a principle of life, freedom, and love that is meant to overflow within us. We are to allow his *in-formation* (in the original, not the modern sense of the word) to make us anew. And we are to allow his teachings to work in us so as to bring about the union of divinity and humanity of which he is the witness.

This does not detract from the pedagogical value of the Torah. The role of external law is one of setting limits, and the ancients often played with the words *horos* and *nomos,* "law" and "limit." Human beings need limits in order to find their form. Children who receive no limits to desire from their parents will have great difficulties in finding and recognizing themselves. And experienced parents can testify that children are actually demanding to be shown limits when they indulge in extreme behavior.

The problem lies in how to give limits that do not confine, distort, or even mutilate the growth and development of a human being. We need both security and freedom for our growth. Some people primarily lack the former, and are bereft of the principles, limits, and grounding they need in order to live with assurance and confidence. Others lack the latter, and remain imprisoned by principles that stifle and block them from living fully.

The Gospel of Mary reminds us that the greatest law is that of love, the love of which Yeshua was the witness. To love, however, is not to be a slave of the law; it is to go beyond the law by fulfilling it. We are not to add more to the law in order accomplish this. Here the Teacher reveals himself as both a Jewish radical and as something quite beyond any such cultural category or label: a fully *human* being.

"Do not add more laws to those given in the Torah . . ."

It was Moses who gave us the essence of the Torah. If this was indeed the same Moshe who was "the humblest man on the face of the earth,"[63] then who are we to add to the laws given through him? The laws are to

---

[63]Nm 12:3.

be lived, not simply followed, and this requires a *thou canst* rather than a *thou shalt*. It is we who have edited and altered the Torah—the teaching that was intended to sustain and free us—and made it into a mere legal code that captures and imprisons us.

Great teachings must always be renewed and reinterpreted so that their essence is still communicated, so that it remains the sap of a living tree. This was the work of the Teacher, who both transmitted and incarnated the Torah—the only work that a messiah, in the true sense of the word, need accomplish. Now, it is we who must accomplish, like him, the Kingdom where his Peace, his Spirit, and the spirit of Anthropos and YHWH reign supreme in ourselves.

> *I AM YHWH, the Presence*
> *who brought you out of Egypt,*
> *the land of servitude.*[64]

I AM is the liberating Presence in each of us, the hidden heart beyond our mechanisms and our addictions. Nothing need be added to this.

> *You are free to have no other gods before Me.*[65]

There is no reality other than Reality. There is no absolute, other than the Absolute. You are free to neither relativize the Absolute, nor "absolutize" the relative. This is the real meaning of idolatry: adoring the creature in the place of the Creator, and created realities rather than the uncreated Reality. There is nothing to be added to this.

You can refrain from making an idol in the form of anything in heaven above, on the earth below, or in the waters. You need not bow

---

[64]Ex 20, for this and following passages. Chouraqui translates this passage as "I am Adonai-YHWH, your Elohim . . ."

[65][This and succeeding passages are not intended to be accurate translations of the commandments of Ex 20, but rather Leloup's exegesis of those passages in the light of Yeshua's teaching about not adding more laws. He systematically substitutes "you may," "you can," or "you are free to" for the Bible's "you shall" or "you must," so as to illustrate his thesis about living the law rather than merely following it.—*Trans.*]

down to these gods, nor serve them, for it is only I who AM. You need not make visible images of the Invisible. You can let the Invisible be invisible, the Transcendent be transcendent, the Intangible be intangible, and the Unnamable be nameless. You can let YHWH, That Which Is, be what It is, in yourself. There is nothing to be added to this.

> *You can refrain from vain utterance of the Name of That Which*
> *Is, Was, and Approaches—YHWH, I AM.*

You may live in wonder and adoration in the presence of the Name of the One who has all names, and whom no name can name. You may allow the One who Is to take whatever name It so pleases within yourself, without this Name becoming your possession or your power; for no name can define or circumscribe It. There is nothing to be added to this.

> *You may honor the day of the Shabbat, and make it a holy day.*

You may rest[66] from all your doing, working, and producing. Human beings are not only made for work, but also for repose—that holy repose that is fully savored after good work, not only on the Sabbath, but every day.

On the day of the Sabbath, all human beings become equal, for there are no more employers and employees. This law is intended to free us from the bounds of another law, that of dominator and dominated. On the Sabbath, there are no more professors and students, no more lords and serfs. There are only the children of God, sons and daughters of the One Light.

You have the right to "be seated in the presence of the One who Is" (another possible meaning of the word *Shabbat*), and to rejoice with your spouse and children, your friends, sisters, and brothers in this Presence. You may honor this day as special, to help keep alive your memory of the essential, and to let go of the worries and contingencies that oppress you.

---

[66]To "rest" or "stop" is the etymological root of the Hebrew word *Shabbat* (Sabbath).

You may openly avow your freedom from the powers, possessions, and knowledge of the world.

Your treasure is the rediscovery of this peace, this pleasure of simply being who you are, a participant in the bliss of Being itself. On the day of Shabbat, you may let go of your ordinary identity of this one or that one, rich or poor, happy or unhappy, in good health or bad health. You may be I AM. There is nothing to be added to this.

You may honor your father and your mother.

You may not love your parents—for love cannot be commanded, though it can be learned through practice. When there is too much bitterness, violence, or coldness, it serves nothing to try to force yourself to love. Yet you can still honor them in the sense of recognizing them in their humanness, whatever their flaws. Whether you like it or not, life has been given to you through them.

To honor your father and mother is also to honor the incarnate reality of your story. This story is what it is, and it is certainly not a perfect one. But if you hope to change it, you will never succeed through denying it and refusing your parents this human respect. Such denial cuts you off from the Real, and may ultimately have serious consequences for your physical and psychic health. Honor your father and mother, and if possible, allow yourself to love them. And especially love them for what they are: fragile, flawed, impermanent human beings who will someday no longer be with you. Any other kind of love risks becoming distorted into dependence or alienation.

The creative intelligence that is the source of this commandment shows real psychological understanding in choosing the word *honor* instead of *love*. As the Teacher himself later elaborated, "Whoever loves their father or their mother more than I AM is incapable of knowing I AM."[67] If we cannot detach ourselves from our family, we lose access to

---

[67]Cf. Mt 10:37; Mk 10:7 and 10:19.

our true identity. Yet access to our true identity also implies an inner reconciliation with the family.

Finally, we cannot truly love the uncreated Source of our being without honoring the created origin of our physical existence. There is nothing to be added to this.

You may refrain from killing.

This does not just mean the use of arms or physical violence—it is also possible to kill through words, even through a look or a thought. With this in mind, we might ask if it really possible for us not to kill. One being's life on this planet is always at the expense of some other form of life. We never cease to kill in order to feed ourselves, whether vegetarian or not. And sometimes, not content with the food on our plate, we indulge an appetite for psychic food by feeding on the ruined reputation of our neighbors. All sorts of strange food sticks to our plate, and our lips are stained with blood. Even more than knives or guns, these signs show the violence in our hearts and the judgment in our minds.

And yet: You may refrain from killing.

As with the other teachings, this is a process of becoming, a road that we are invited to walk upon, a process of radical transformation of our entire being. It would of course take an inspired and mighty effort to imagine a believable society that is not founded on murder, on self-assertion at the expense of someone else, and the many other forms of destruction of others in the name of survival. Doesn't Darwin tell us that this is a law of evolution—survival of those who are the strongest and most capable of adapting to circumstances?

But which evolution? Is it the evolution of ever more neocortex cunning in service to the reptilian core of the old brain, or the evolution of the entire brain as a holistic instrument capable of peace, harmony, and the higher perception of which the Teacher speaks?

"You may refrain from killing" is an evolutionary teaching that makes technological progress a servant of the process of our humanization, instead of a mere instrument of our animal heritage. There is nothing to be added to this.

You may refrain from adultery.

The original meaning of adultery is betrayal of the Real, of lying to oneself by knowingly allowing a reflection to usurp the place of the Light itself or, in other words, idolatry.

But as human beings, we have the capacity to refrain from being slaves to our impulses, instincts, and emotions, and of our thoughts and ideas. You may choose a woman (or a man) over others; but this need not involve a sense of exclusion or rejection of others. It manifests our capacity of choice, yet a choice that includes both a certain fidelity and a certain freedom with regard to the impulses and emotions that both animate and distract us.

This commandment means above all to refrain from regarding a partner in a way that indulges our craving or makes him or her into an object or a tool at our service. Adultery exists in the very heart of even a monogamous marriage when a partner is regarded in this way. We are unfaithful to our partner when we cease to see him or her as one who has the same birthright of freedom as ourselves. We deceive a partner when we make him or her into an object, and we deceive ourselves when we call this love.

But you may abandon this atmosphere of lies and adultery. You may love others for who they are, whether you keep your vow to them or refuse to make it. Nothing and no one can force you to stay with someone, nor force you to leave them.

"What God has joined together, let man not separate."[68] It is clear that when two beings are truly united in love, then nothing can separate them (not even marriage!). The truth of their relationship remains the truth, whether they recognize it or not and whether they live separately or together. The truth of love cannot be identified with (and thereby reduced

---

[68]Mk 10:9.

to) the emotional state of being "in love." It is precisely at those moments when this "in love" feeling is gone that only the truth of love can enable us to really *choose* love. This choice is also the real meaning of faithfulness, a transcendent demeanor that cannot be defined by rules, conditions, and time.

"What God has joined together, let man not separate"—but only if it is God who has done the joining![69] You may refrain from living in adultery by remaining faithful to that which sometimes occurs between two beings and is often called love. This invites us to discover something that is not only sacred, but ultimately far more interesting than the spectacle of our impulses, our emotional intensities—or worse, our obedience to duty.

"In the beginning, God created the Human in his image . . . Male and female were created by him." This passage from Genesis 1:27 means, among other things, that in the heart of a conscious and loving relationship we are invited to experience a love that is not of time and the convoluted paths of our passing loves. There is nothing to be added to this.

You may refrain from stealing.

The deeper meaning of this is about greed. Can we not be happy with what comes to us, instead of wanting what others have? Chapter 20 of Exodus elaborates further: You can be free from desiring your neighbor's house, wife, servants, cow, or donkey. You can be free of all desire for that which belongs to your neighbor. Moses shows no lack of imagination here—and, like the Teacher, an incredible optimism in the faith that some day human beings will not only be capable of refraining from theft, but from desire and envy!

This presupposes a true *metanoia*, a transformation of consciousness. It demands that human beings find within themselves the Source of true happiness and satisfaction, so that there is no longer any pressure that might foster envy or the desire to steal. It implies a return to one's true

[69]For more on this question, see the publication *Evidences paradoxales*, interview with Jean-Yves Leloup by M. de Solemne (Editions du Fennec, 1996).

center, the divine I AM, the source of all value. It is also the source of an abundant energy that empowers us to work effectively, not only for our own needs, but for those of others.

But human beings are capable of much more than freedom from greed and theft—they are also capable of sharing and giving. It is no accident that those who harbor envy and greed are so rarely happy and that the only authentic smiles we still can find in this world are from those who give and share. By reminding us of this evolutionary potential, Moses and Yeshua after him are also inviting us to live with greater joy and less sadness. What more can be added to this?

You may refrain from bearing false witness against your neighbor.

The deeper meaning of these words is this: You have the capacity to stop all your lying. But this implies a highly evolved state of consciousness. It means that we no longer dwell in our projections, that we see others as they are, without adding or subtracting anything.

What is, is. What is not, is not. This teaching of Yeshua is also found in other traditions.[70] Anything added to this is "of the Devil"—some would translate this as "of the Liar," others as "of the discursive mind." This enjoins us to see things as they are, without ulterior motives, without self-deception, without discursive thought . . . but is this really possible? If so, then it can be only when we are able to look at someone or something with total innocence—without the summation of our accumulated memories or the projection of memory, and therefore judgment.

Is not this innocence of regard the same as that of a pure and peaceful heart? The ancient sages said that we shall be judged by the regard of a child. Unfortunately, not all children have such total innocence. From birth on, their regard is loaded and conditioned by memories—perhaps through the genetic code itself. Hence their regard already may be some-

---

[70]See Jean-Yves Leloup, *L'Enracinement et l'Ouverture* (Paris: Albin Michel). [For an interesting compendium of sayings of Jesus from other traditions, see Marvin Mayer, *The Unknown Sayings of Jesus* (San Francisco: Harper, 1998).—*Trans.*]

what mentally loaded—certainly with less baggage than that of most adults, but with baggage nonetheless.

Perhaps only those who have encountered the regard of a saint or a sage, totally free of all projections, know what it really means to be capable of not bearing false witness. We have been seeing others and ourselves through perceptions based on lies. In regarding others, the number of mental associations from the past varies greatly among us—sometimes we may feel a certain richness in such memories, yet it is this very richness that often prevents us from simply seeing others, from seeing what is.

One of the Teacher's closest companions said: "We shall see God as he Is, for we shall have become like unto him."[71]

As God Is—not as we think of, imagine, or represent God. We can see only that which we are like. To know both the Divine and the human as they truly are is to become like unto both. There is nothing to be added to this.

The entire Torah of Moses can be summarized in this great exercise that the Teacher reminds us of:

> You shall love the Lord your God
> with all your heart, with all your strength,
> and with all your mind.
> You shall love your neighbor as yourself.[72]

When was it that someone told us this means, "You *must* love"? Since when have we been able to love on command? When we accepted such a command, we became as hypocritical as it is possible for a human to be. The teaching of love has never been you *must*, you *should*. The teaching has always been you *can*—you can love, you shall love, not only with all your heart, but also with all your mind and strength. You can love with all

---

[71][This is the author's résumé of 1 Jn 3:2.—*Trans.*]
[72]See Dt 6:5.

your being, rediscovering in this very act of love your own wholeness, your own divine-human nature.

There is no obligation here—and that is what is so difficult for us. The only thing that YHWH cannot do is oblige us to love. Love cannot be forced, but only aroused, called by desire.

This is why Emmanuel (meaning "God with us") is the very desire we feel for him, this desire to love him with all our intelligence, feeling, and force. And it is why Emmanuel is also the desire to love our neighbor as we love ourselves. Finally, it is only through knowing the love of God that we are able truly to love ourselves.

There is in us this potential and this longing to love the other as YHWH loves the other, this longing to allow I AM to love us and to allow ourselves to love one another. As that great dreamer, Paul of Tarsus, said, after being blinded by the clear light on that famous road to Damascus: May God become the all in All.[73] There is nothing to be added to this. To elaborate upon such words is to detract from them. Yet in the place of this great law of life, we have substituted all sorts of little rules, conventions, and contraventions that poison life, corrupt desire, and grieve the holy Breath. This is why the Teacher warned us to "impose no law"—that is, "do not impose the projections of your individual ego or of the collective ego of society . . . other than that which I have witnessed" (other than the Torah, and the love, intelligence, and freedom that Yeshua embodied). Do not add to what Moses was able to transmit, for there is nothing to be added to it.

Do not become the slaves of the laws you have imposed upon yourselves and upon others. Neither become the slaves of the laws written in your very genes and flesh, for you were created to evolve, to advance not toward that sterile, negative void, but toward the divine and fertile emptiness.

You can dwell in openness, an opening of spirit, heart, and body wherein the holy Breath rejoices. Dwell in freedom *even as* I dwell in free-

---

[73]See 1 Cor 15:28.

dom. I am with you unto the end of the worlds.[74] I AM.

[Page 9, continued]

5   *Having said all this, he departed.*

6   *The disciples were in sorrow,*

7   *shedding many tears, and saying:*

8   *"How are we to go among the unbelievers*

9   *and announce the gospel of the Kingdom of the Son of*
      Man?

10   *They did not spare his life,*

11   *so why should they spare ours?"*

This reaction of the disciples to the departure of the Teacher shows that his peace had not become established in them, that his teachings had not yet been fully integrated, and that fear and loss were still basic, unhappy constituents of their emotional nature.

The "old man" of whom Paul speaks is still active in them. Yeshua's information has not yet become transformation. Yet surely it is only human, a natural reaction of any psychic being, to shed tears at the departure of a friend.

Nevertheless, the Gospel of Mary seems to be telling us that there is something other than human nature at work in the disciples, which affects their motivation. They are afraid to announce the Good News to unbelievers, afraid of being persecuted as the Teacher was persecuted. It is from this fear that he desired to free them when he said, "Walk forth, those persecuted for justice's sake!"[75]

In the light of Pneuma, the spiritual Reality in which Yeshua was inviting the disciples to live, persecution becomes an opportunity for growth in consciousness and love. This seems to have escaped most of

---

[74]See Mt 28:20.

[75]Mt 5, Chouraqui translation; see also Jn 15:20: "If they have persecuted me, they will also persecute you."

them, but it certainly does not escape the one whom they have tended to regard as a "weak woman." In the hour of adversity, Miriam of Magdala proves herself to have the most strength, faith, endurance, resolution, and hope in her suffering of the crucifixion of their master and friend.

Mark, Matthew, and the other evangelists make a point of noting the continued presence of women at Golgotha, long after the men had fled:

> Many women were there, watching from a distance. They had
> followed Jesus from Galilee to care for his needs.
> Among them were Mary Magdalene, Mary the mother of
> James and Joseph, and the mother of Zebedee's sons.[76]

Are men less courageous than women? Perhaps they have less fear of death, but more fear of suffering? There are no simple answers to this. Yet it is worth noting that it is often mostly women who are present in great moments of life such as this, at deathbed and at birth. Husbands and fathers are more often absent. Surely this should not be seen as desertion (of which they are sometimes accused), but rather as an indication of the great difficulty that the masculine mind (and some feminine minds as well) experiences when it feels powerless in the face of a suffering that it can neither combat nor alleviate. If there were only something to *do*, some action to be taken, some arms or tools to be used, the masculine mind could tell itself that man was more useful and effective.

The feminine mind (and again, this includes some men as well) surely has an advantage when it comes to dealing with this feeling of power-lessness and uselessness in the face of certain kinds of suffering. It is more capable of simply being present and bearing witness in patience and com-passion—for this is a different kind of usefulness and power, one that is closer to the world of Pneuma of which Yeshua himself was the Witness.

We must also remember that for Peter, James, John, and the other dis-

---

[76]Mt 27:55.

ciples, going among the unbelievers also meant rubbing shoulders with the *goyim*, the pagans and heretics, the impure. For pious and faithful Jews, this was not only disagreeable, it also implied a kind of renunciation of an elect status. But the Teacher had shown them that the divine lineage was not the exclusive privilege of a specific people, but of all those who dare to open their minds and hearts to the teachings of the Living One.

For Peter, a great vision was needed for him to understand that "God does not show favoritism, but welcomes those of every nation who do what is right and who seek and love him."[77]

The next day, as they approached the city, Peter went up to the rooftop about the sixth hour, in order to pray.

He felt hungry and asked for something to eat, but as his food was being prepared he fell into ecstasy. He saw the sky open up and an object like a huge cloth being lowered to earth by its four corners. Inside the cloth were all sorts of four-footed animals, reptiles, and all kind of birds of the air.

A voice then spoke: "Get up, Peter. Sacrifice, and eat."

But Peter replied, "But no, Lord, I have never eaten anything so dirty and impure."

Again, the voice spoke: "Do not call impure what God has purified." This was said three times, and the object was then carried back to the sky.

Greatly perplexed, Peter was wondering what this vision could mean, when at that moment some men sent by Cornelius arrived at his house. They inquired of those below if this was indeed the house of Simon, known as Peter, and asked if he were there.

While he was still reflecting upon his vision, the Spirit said to him: "Three men are here looking for you. Go downstairs and go with them with no misgivings, for it is I who have sent them."

Peter went down to them and said: "I am the man you are looking for. Why have you come to me?"

---

[77][This is a free translation of Acts 10:34–35. Conventional translations say "those who fear him," and Chouraqui says "those whom he makes tremble."—*Trans.*]

They answered: "The centurion Cornelius, a just and God-fearing man, respected by all Jews, has been told by a holy angel to bring you to his house so he may hear your words."

Then Peter bade them enter, and gave them hospitality.

The next day he went off with them, accompanied by some of the brothers from Joppa. They arrived at Caesarea the following day. Cornelius was waiting for them, along with his family and close friends. He began to kneel down and bow, but Peter said: "Stand up. I am only a man myself."

As he came into the room, talking to Cornelius, he saw that there were many people gathered there, and said to them:

"You are well aware that it is against our law for a Jew to visit and associate with Gentiles like this. But God has shown me that I should not call any person impure or unclean."[78]

So we see that the disciples are being asked to overcome this prohibition and thereby renounce their status of being in the elect. For the male religious mind, this is not an easy thing to do.

At this point, we need to clarify the meaning of the word *elect*, for this has been used not only to apply to the Jews as "chosen people," but also by Christians, and centuries later, by Moslems as well. Today there is still no lack of groups who make this claim, calling themselves "the last of the just," "the new and final chosen ones," "the born-again," and so forth.

What does it mean to be "chosen?" This recalls the story of the old rabbi who said, "God chose us because we were the least spiritual, the most wanton and stubborn of peoples, stiff-necked and slow to believe. So if we are the elect, then other groups must be even more so, if they are less proud and slow to believe than we are."

The rabbi's words echo those of Paul of Tarsus: "If God has chosen me, a persecutor and a criminal, then certainly he has chosen you, who

---

[78]Acts 10:9–28.

have not killed and persecuted." We could go even further back to David, the messiah-king, to find yet another example. Was he not an adulterer and criminal who sent Uriah to die because he wanted Uriah's wife, Bathsheba, even though he already had a large harem of concubines?[79]

God does not choose us as a people or as individuals because of our worthiness, but because of an overflowing of love that transcends our simple human ethics without denying them. In exactly that area where we feel most condemned by human judgment, there appears another resource, a different kind of conscience, which knows us as we are, however sordid or pleasant the appearances.

But the words *elect* or *chosen* are not always understood in this sense, and this has unfortunately given rise to an interpretation tainted by arrogance of the elect toward those who are not of the chosen group. This is clearly the basis of Yeshua's critique of those with whom he shared the same lineage, traditions, and faith. Just as he could be so kind to those whom Jews called "sinners," he could be very harsh with the self-righteous: "You believe yourselves righteous among men, but YHWH, the One Who Is, knows your hearts. That which men hold supreme is an abomination in the Presence of YHWH, the One Who Is."[80]

These words recall the famous story of the Pharisee and the tax-collector:

> *Two men went up into the temple to pray, one a Pharisee and*
> *the other a tax collector.*
> *The Pharisee stood and prayed thus with himself, "God, I*
> *thank thee that I am not like other men, extortioners, unjust,*
> *adulterers, or even like this tax collector.*
> *I fast twice a week, and I give tithes of all that I get."*
> *But the tax collector, standing far off, would not even lift up*

---

[79]2 Sam 11–12.

[80][The author's rendering of Lk 16:15. Chouraqui gives simply "Elohim" rather than "YHWH, the One Who Is."—*Trans.*]

*his eyes to heaven, but beat his breast, saying, "God, be merciful
to me a sinner!"
I tell you, it is this man went down to his house justified rather
than the other; for every one who exalts himself will be
humbled, but he who humbles himself will be exalted.*[81]

Yet we might sometimes be tempted to reverse things for the contemporary scene, where there are now so many who stand at a distance and beat their breasts loudly for their sins in order to display their humility and make themselves feel better—Pharisees wearing the masks of tax collectors!

At any rate, we can see that the disciples as portrayed in the Gospel of Mary have not yet found the peace and freedom of the Son of Man within themselves. They are not yet able to walk forth and announce his gospel to all. They fear suffering at some level, whether of body, mind, or reputation. But the Teacher has already foreseen the trials of his disciples:

*If the world hates you, know that it has hated me before it
hated you. . . .
Truly, truly, I say to you, you will weep and lament, but the
world will rejoice; you will be sorrowful, but your sorrow will
turn into joy.
When a woman is in labor she has sorrow, because her hour has
come; but when she is delivered of the child, she no longer
remembers the anguish, for joy that a human being
[Anthropos] has been born into the world.*[82]

It is Miriam of Magdala who serves the disciples as a midwife, not of body or soul, but of that eternal Son whose Presence seeks to reveal itself in the very heart of that which trembles most within them.

[81]Lk 18:9–14.
[82]Jn 15:18; and Jn 16:20–21.

[Page 9, continued]

12   *Then Mary arose,*

13   *embraced them all, and began to speak to her brothers:*

14   *"Do not remain in sorrow and doubt,*

15   *for his Grace will guide you and comfort you."*

As her brothers despair, Mary rises (*anastasis* in the Greek). It was she who had first seen Christ himself risen from the dead, and his strength so fills her that she is able to console and warmly embrace them all. Her tears and tenderness are not reserved for her beloved apart from others, for this love knows no exclusion and is offered in purity of heart to be shared by all. This demonstrates a simplicity of contact and relationship that is typical of the earliest Christian communities. In their sharing of faith, their memories of Yeshua and his teachings, and their very bread, they include the body in a non-dualistic vision of oneness with the living Christ.

"Do not remain in sorrow and doubt . . ."

A more literal translation might be "Do not be sad, and do not have a divided heart."[83] As in other gospels, sadness and doubt imply indecision, the hesitation that weakens and destroys faith.[84] Those of divided heart and mind live in a duality that can lead to a kind of schizophrenia or internal split—actions are in conflict with words, words with thoughts, and thoughts with desires. Their desires no longer express their being, and that being is estranged from its source in Being. Once again harmony is shattered and there is anguish and war between the human being and his or her self-image.

"Let man not separate what God has united." This theme, which recurs often in early Christian texts before Constantine, urges us not to

---

[83]Coptic snaudia, which corresponds to Greek dispsukos, or dipsukia, "to have two souls," "to have two psyches."

[84]See Lk 8:52; Mt 21:21; and Mk 11:23.

live in the torments of *dipsukia* (duplicity of soul). When we are able to see opposites as complementary we have taken a step toward oneness with the Son, or if you prefer, toward true maturity.[85]

One salient characteristic of early Judeo-Christian spirituality is the importance given to *aplótès*,[86] or "simplicity of soul," as contrasted with dipsukia. Because the latter involves convolutions and twists of memories with which we identify, it is the work of an entire lifetime to find the path of simplicity of soul. Miriam, in her confident and passionate abiding with the Presence of the Teacher, becomes simple in this sense, for she practices and embodies his teachings. She is able to console and strengthen the wavering step of her brothers by reminding them that the grace of Yeshua accompanies and protects them. She shows them that they will not go far by relying on their personal strength and abilities apart from the Source. On the other hand if they stay with the Source, they will know that something other is at work in them. A lightness, a grace, even a gratuitousness (these two words have the same etymology) reigns at the heart of their very real problems and reckonings. This lightness both enlivens and truly protects them.

There is certainly insufficient protection for our body, with its delicate immune system, when the soul has lost its confidence. Divisions in the soul weaken the body, whereas confidence and simplicity (aplótès) restore its strength and integrity. Though the Gospel of Mary is not a medical treatise, it does remind us of the serious consequences to the physical body—and to the social and cosmic bodies that surround and penetrate it—when human desire becomes disoriented, losing its "unwrinkled" bond to the presence of Being. This can be cured only by a rediscovery of fundamental confidence in the Anthropos that lives within us. It is this which makes communion between our mortal and immortal natures possible.

---

[85]See footnote 83. Among other early Christian texts, see the First Epistle of Clement 11:2 and the Epistle of Barnaby 19:5.

[86]*Aplótès*, from the Greek "without folds," "unwrinkled," "unconvoluted."

[Page 9, continued]

16   *"Instead, let us praise his greatness,*

17   *for he has prepared us for this.*

18   *He is calling upon us to become fully human [Anthropos]."*

19   *Thus Mary turned their hearts toward the Good,*

20   *and they began to discuss the meaning of the Teacher's*
        words.

In the face of adversity, with fear and dissension among the disciples, Mary reminds them of the unifying power of praise:

"Instead, let us praise his greatness . . ."

As long as we are able to praise God for being God, whether manifest or unmanifest, the seeds of peace will be able to grow in us.

But the space for praise and gratitude that we withhold in ourselves will be quickly taken over by doubt or sadness—in old-fashioned language, by the Devil, the Diabolos, meaning the divider who introduces dualism into us.

This does not imply any sort of willed gaiety or joy. Praise, like worship (which is silent praise), is a way of restoring things to their proper place, of reconnecting with a sense of value and discrimination as to what is truly essential for our life and what is not. In the present situation, Miriam asks the disciples to center themselves in the greatness of God, rather than in their small, troubled selves. This is to leave egocentrism and return to theocentrism.

The ancients sometimes said that the worst sin is ingratitude, which is a forgetting of the greatness, beauty, truth, and goodness of the Source that is constantly creating us—in other terms, a forsaking of Being, and of the Good.

And yet,

". . . he has prepared us for this."

His mission and teaching among us was a ceaseless recollection, using both ancient scriptures and entirely new situations, of that which is our true nature:

"He is calling upon us to become **fully human.***"*

This way of translating the deep significance of Anthropos, which we discussed earlier, reminds us of that *archetype of synthesis* that the Teacher himself incarnated. Irenaeus, following John, said that "he became a man so as to show human beings what being human really means, in the image and likeness of God."[87] We are this Anthropos—both "already" and "not yet"— just as the acorn is both already and not yet the oak tree in all its splendor.

This recalls logion 114 from the Gospel of Thomas:

> *Simon Peter said to him:*
> *"Let Mary leave us,*
> *for women are not fit for the Life."*
> *Jesus answered:*
> *"See, I have been guiding her*
> *so as to make her into a human* [Anthropos].
> *She, too, will become*
> *a living breath, like you.*
> *Any woman who becomes a human*
> *will enter the Kingdom of God."*[88]

---

[87]Irenaeus of Lyon, *Adversus Haereses* III, 18:7.
[88]See Jean-Yves Leloup, *L'Evangile de Thomas* (Paris: Albin Michel, 1986), 243.

The error of many translators is to render this as having something to do with being male. It is clear from the original Greek that the meaning is that of *anthropos* (human being in the general sense), and not of *andros* (man in the masculine sense). It is true that in order to become whole, a human being must integrate in herself or himself the complementary gender. And this work or realization of wholeness is certainly not something that only or especially women have to do—we each have our own work of becoming an Anthropos, a fully *human* being.

Among the various texts of ancient Christianity, we might also mention the writings of the Pseudo-Clementine Homelies, as well as those of Theodotus and Asclepius, all of whom identify the Kingdom as presence of the Anthropos in his or her full humanness.[89]

These texts also speak of the "inner" or "essential" Man—the *ontos Anthropos*. For Jacques Ménard, the most suggestive example would seem to be that passage from the *Pistis Sophia* where Mary Magdalene is said to feel this inner human in herself, and when she identifies this as her true self, she understands everything.[90]

The term *anthropos* is also richer than the term *androgyne*, which is sometimes used as the translation of the former, for sexual and psychic polarities form only a part of what must be integrated in becoming fully human.

This recalls a passage from the Gospel of Matthew:

> *But he said to them, "Not all men can receive this saying, but only those to whom it is given.*
> *For there are eunuchs who have been so from birth, and there are eunuchs who have been made eunuchs by men, and there are eunuchs who have made themselves eunuchs for the sake of*

---

[89]See *Homélies pseudo-clémentines* II, 15:3. See passages from Theodotus 21:2–3, and from Asclepius VII, 8 cited by J. E. Ménard in his *Evangile de Thomas* (Leiden: E. J. Brill, 1975), 210.

[90]*Pistis Sophia* 113, 189, quoted by Ménard in his *Evangile de Thomas*, 210. For an English translation of this scripture, see C. Schmidt, *Pistis Sophia* (NHS 9, 460–87), tran. V. MacDermot (Leiden: E. J. Brill, 1978).

the Kingdom of heaven. He who is able to receive this, let him receive it."[91]

Some scholars have detected here the hand of an editor who was influenced by some sort of dualistic or ascetic teaching, one that was to influence Christianity's monastic departure from Old Testament teachings. Indeed, it does seem implausible that Yeshua would advocate destroying the work of the Creator. How could he who claimed to be One with the Father advocate such mutilation of his creatures?

Others explain this by an improper translation or transmission of Yeshua's words. The word *eunuch* should be replaced by the word *androgyne*. Unfortunately the latter word (like so many others) was and still is often misunderstood and reduced to a sexual meaning that evokes some sort of freakish bisexual mixture that is neither male nor female—hardly an advantage for someone who is already having difficulties in finding his or her identity!

As in so many other domains, one can only transcend that which one has fully known and accepted. One must live one's own sexuality in one's own body before speaking of a higher state of androgyny. As in psychotherapy, one must first have an ego that is as sane and stable as possible before pretending to have access to what is often (perhaps too often) called the Self.

This is why the authors of the Gospel of Mary considered it so important that Yeshua really lived his masculine sexuality, perhaps with Miriam, perhaps with another woman. This was necessary in order for him to become the archetype of synthesis, the Anthropos that he was. I prefer the term *anthropos* to *androgyne* because the former word still leads to confusion today, in spite of a widespread contemporary appreciation of the value of spiritual integration and balance of male and female polarities in us. Rather than defending the literal translation of the original word used in certain early Christian texts, it is preferable here to defend,

---

[91]Mt 19:11–12.

through the word we choose as its translation, the truth and richness of meaning in what the original word communicates.

What is important is to become whole. This is what makes us able to truly love, not from our sense of lack, but from our plenitude, as Yeshua himself loved us.

In the same way, we can say that it is because Miriam of Magdala fully lives her feminine sexuality, and because she fully accepts and integrates the masculine dimension of her being, that she is able to speak with authentic knowledge of the Word—though today, as during her time, there are still those who would deny her this. But it is only after the long and slow work of becoming fully human that she can legitimately speak, as an Anthropos, of the fullness of a humanity that, like Yeshua's, is open to the Divine and transparent to its clear light—the most invisible and subtle of lights.

> *Thus Mary turned their hearts toward the Good . . .*

Her words are a recollection of the essential. Inviting the disciples to abandon vain talk and false rhetoric, she turns their hearts toward the Good, reorienting their minds and desires towards that living Anthropos within them to which the Teacher had urged them to bear witness.

> *. . . and they began to discuss the meaning of the Teacher's words.*

His words are a lamp shining upon the darkness of the road. Together, they enlighten each other by discussing them. Like the disciples on the road to Emmaus, they hear and feel the meaning of the words: *Did our hearts not burn within us while he talked to us on the road, and opened the scriptures to us?*[92]

---

[92]Lk 24:32.

[Page 10]

1   *Peter said to Mary:*

2   *"Sister, we know that the Teacher loved you*

3   *differently from other women.*

4   *Tell us whatever you remember*

5   *of any words he told you*

6   *which we have not yet heard."*

Having been consoled and had his spirits restored by Miriam, Peter now asks her to reveal the Teacher's words known to her alone. His attitude suggests a certain deference and respect for her, both because of her special intimacy with Yeshua, and because of the peace of the Son of Man that she has just manifested. This deference, however, is not to last for long when she actually began to comply with his request. . . .

The character of Miriam of Magdala as revealed in this gospel is fascinating, and deserves an entire study in itself. Nevertheless, we must also consider her in the context of how the other gospels, and early Christianity in general, viewed her.

Some scholars have argued that there are three different Marys in the gospels: Mary the sinner, Mary of Bethany, and Mary Magdalene. Whatever conclusion we may draw, their arguments are not irrelevant, for the stories of these three Marys are indeed those of three different women. But according to the ancient exegesis, this does not literally mean three women, but one woman depicted at different stages of her evolution: sinner, contemplative, and intimate friend of Yeshua.

Miriam is, in fact, much more than three women. Just as she is capable of embodying seven demonic aspects of femininity by obstructing (*shatan*, in Hebrew) the manifestation of Being through dividing it (diabolos), she is equally capable of embodying seven angelic—or at least more fully human—aspects of femininity as she draws ever nearer to the Anthropos, the Man-God embodied by her teacher.

Thus we see that the early exegetes gave priority to an archetypal reading of Miriam's words, deeds, and gestures. Making use of the canonical Gospels, they considered her as a feminine archetype at work in all human beings, and one whose mutations can shed light on each person's path.

We can distinguish at least seven images, or feminine archetypes, that come into play in the specific scenes from the canonical Gospels where Miriam appears. A major one is the archetype of the lover whose desire is disoriented or disturbed. This interpretation of the repentant sinner whom we find at Yeshua's feet in Simon the Pharisee's house[93] has become the dominant popular image of recent centuries—yet there is nothing in the passage itself about the nature of her sin.

We have already noted that her transgression could also be related to her thirst for knowledge, her desire to engage in studies reserved for men only in those days. This would certainly be enough to make her a dangerous woman, even an outlaw. Curiously enough, there is nothing in any of the four Gospels that states that she was ever a prostitute. Of course, lust might be one of the seven possessing demons of which Yeshua cures her. If so, it certainly isn't the only one, nor the deadliest. The canonical Gospels offer no information as to the specific nature of the seven demons or spirits that initially possess Miriam—that is to say, alienate her from her freedom. However, we might make some surmises about them by referring to other texts that were current in those times. According to Evagrius Ponticus, who made a thorough study of such matters,[94] these *logismoï* (his term for "negative or destructive thoughts") act to destroy a person's orientation toward the nous, and then the orientation of the nous toward the Pneuma. In other words, they act to obstruct peace, contemplation, and the Presence of the Son seeking to establish itself in the person. Lists of such demonic spirits vary. In the West they later become known as the seven deadly or cardinal sins: gluttony, fornication, covetousness, sadness,

---

[93]See Lk 7:36–50.

[94]Evagre le Pontique, *Praxis et gnosis,* French translation by Jean-Yves Leloup (Paris: Albin Michel). In English, see Evagrius Ponticus, *Praktikos* (Cistercian Press, 1980).

anger, vainglory, pride.[95] Evagrius adds *accidie* [96] to the list, meaning a kind of despondency or apathetic rejection of spiritual realities.

Such negative thought forms (logismoï) make human beings ill, and this sickness is indeed a kind of possession, which can also be interpreted as pathologies that cause alienation from our true nature—such as oral, anal, and genital fixations (which are often linked to vices such as greed, violent temper, and so forth). They are the elements of the pathology of the ego, which is centered upon itself and its own pleasure and gratification. Only an awakening to authentic love—which is also an encounter with the Other (i.e., the Real)—can deliver us from such possession.

In the *Corpus Hermeticum,*[97] it is said that these demons are the malignant offspring of our harmful actions. They are like torturers whose punishment is intended to drive us back to awareness:

> The first torturer is ignorance; the second is sadness; the third is self-indulgence; the fourth is lust; the fifth is injustice; the sixth is greed; the seventh deceitfulness; the eighth craving; the ninth fraud; the tenth anger; the eleventh haste; the twelfth ill will.[98]

Here we have twelve demons instead of seven— the number is not so important, for there are endless ways of analyzing the incredible forms of suffering of which human beings are capable, all of which block their simplicity and peace of mind. We might note that all these lists of demons or pathologies would seem to have some sort of relation to the Ten Commandments of the Torah, describing the unhappy consequences of making bad use of one's freedom.

Let us now turn to the Shepherd of Hermas and the *Testaments of the Apostolic Fathers*, a text contemporary with the canonical Gospels:

---

[95][Leloup's list is somewhat different from the traditional list in English, which is: pride, lust, envy, anger, covetousness, gluttony, and sloth.—*Trans.*]

[96]English *accidie,* French *acédie,* from Greek *akedia.*

[97]See *Corpus hermeticum* (Festugière); in English, see Salaman, et. al., *The Way of Hermes: New Translations of the Corpus Hermeticum* (Rochester, Vt.: Inner Traditions, 2000), 67.

[98]Festugière, traité XIII, 203.

Slander is a turbulent demon [. . . .] Keep far away from him. Presumptuousness and complacency are a powerful demon. Anger is a very malicious spirit. Covetousness is a savage one, and very difficult to tame. Doubt is an earthly spirit that is of the devil. And sadness is the most harmful of all the spirits.[99]

Thus, even though the Gospels do not specify Miriam of Magdala's demons, we have grounds for trying to learn something by imagining them. Undoubtedly there are demons or pathologies peculiar to the male or female sex. The most useful thing for us to know is the power of our own shadow. Without this knowledge, any of us is capable of being taken over by the worst of our worst aspects, and finding ourselves behaving in a fashion that is rightly called inhuman.

The presence of incarnate love frees Miriam from these powers that are said to have inhabited her. She feels recognized, yet not judged, in the very darkness of her shadow. After this, the luminous dimensions of her being can awaken within her. This is what gives her access to the best of her best aspects, which allows her to become fully human, rather than taking the road that ultimately leads to the inhuman. Even more, she enters the path of becoming an Anthropos herself, in the image of the One who has truly loved her in her entirety.

This enables her to embody another feminine archetype—that of the contemplative, dwelling in a ground of silence, listening with total attention to the Teacher.[100] From this contemplation, compassion can then be born. Miriam was thus to become the feminine archetype of spiritual intercession, often to aid sick and dying people. In fact, with her prayers, she participated in the revival of her brother Lazarus.[101]

This contemplation and compassion leads her little by little toward that visionary gift that manifests in her foreknowledge of the impending

---

[99] *Testaments des douze patriarches*, in *Der Hirt des Hermas*, 518–19. In English, see *The Shepherd of Hermas*, Loeb Classical Library, no. 25 (Cambridge, Mass.: Harvard University Press, 1964).

[100] See Lk 10:38–42.

[101] See Jn 11:1–46.

death of Yeshua.[102] She follows him to the cross and as far as death itself, and is the first to see him in his risen form. Her presence at his death on the cross[103] also suggests the archetype of the midwife who accompanies others in their great passages, especially that of death. Furthermore, because she accompanies him at his death she is able, in a sense, to accompany him beyond death and be privileged as the first witness of the Resurrection. It is as such that she has been called "the apostle of apostles,"[104] whose mission is to announce the Good News ("gospel," or *euangelion*) of the love that is stronger than death.

Through this process of initiation she ultimately becomes the Sophia wedded to the Logos, the revealer of mysteries. This aspect of Miriam, though only suggested in the canonical Gospels, are quite developed in the gospels of Thomas, of Philip, and of Mary. It is our feeling, however, that we should not dissociate this grand and ultimate archetypal aspect of Miriam of Magdala from the other faces of the feminine that she embodies, from the most physical to the most spiritual. This would do an injustice to the long road of healing and integration that she symbolizes. It would be like cutting up the robe that the Teacher intended for her to wear—a seamless one like his own.

I noted in the introduction that in the Gospel of Philip, for example, that she is presented as the literal consort of Yeshua—he often "kissed her on the mouth" (*nashak,* in Hebrew). In Jewish tradition this can also mean a sharing of the same breath or spirit, and hence the same Word and gnosis.

Philip's gospel also tells us that Miriam is Christ's sister and mother as well as his companion (koinonos).[105] She is not confined to a single role

---

[102]Her "prophetic" gesture of anointing his feet in Jn 12:1–8.

[103]See Mt 27:55–56.

[104]See Jn 20:11–18. [This title has sometimes been edited as "apostle *to* the apostles" in order to diminish her status to one of subservience to the others.—*Trans.*]

[105]See Robinson, *The Nag Hammadi Library;* and Willis Barnstone, ed., *The Other Bible* (San Francisco: HarperSan Francisco, 1980). See also Ménard, trans and ed., *L'Evangile selon Philippe* (Strasbourg, 1967), for specific passages: 6–11; 63; 34–64; 59, 62.

in her relationship with Yeshua. He is also her *rabbuni*, as mentioned in John 20:16. Rather than continuing to translate this as merely "my rabbi" or "my master," it would be more accurate, in this light, to render this as "my beloved master," with all the tenderness, intimacy, and respect implied by such words.

After Christ has died, it is this woman whom Peter addresses with deference, recognizing that the Teacher had loved her differently from them and from other women. Perhaps this also contains at least a grain of recognition that she has been given teachings that the men have not been ready to hear—for in spite of her status as a mere woman, she has gone farther upon the path to becoming fully human, an Anthropos.

> *"Tell us whatever you remember*
> *of any words he told you*
> *which we have not yet heard."*

[Page 10, continued]

7   *Mary said to them:*

8   *"I will now speak to you*

9   *of that which has not been given to you to hear.*

10   *I had a vision of the Teacher,*

11   *and I said to him:*

12   *'Lord I see you now*

13   *in this vision.'*

14   *And he answered:*

15   *'You are blessed, for the sight of me does not disturb you.*

16   *There where is the nous, lies the treasure.'"*

Peter has asked Miriam for *words* of the teacher that they have not *heard*. Yet she chooses to answer him in terms of a vision she has received:

"I will now speak to you
of that which has not been given to you to hear.
I had a vision . . ."

This deliberate shift from the auditory to the visual will come as no surprise to scholars of early Christianity and the Judaism of Yeshua's time. It is related to an ancient argument as to the primacy of vision over audition. It would be tempting, though simplistic, to conclude that Semitic peoples tend more toward audition (*Shema Yisraël*, "Listen, O Israel!") and Greeks toward vision. What position did the earliest Christians take in this debate as to the favored organ of divine perception?

According to certain texts attributed to the apostle John, it would seem that vision is privileged: "The life appeared; we have *seen* it and testify to it." And he has Yeshua himself say: "Your father Abraham rejoiced at the thought of *seeing* my day. He *saw* it and was glad."[106] Thus vision would be the fulfillment of the promise of audition, its plenitude and joy. One could read the Gospel of Mary as saying that Peter and the others have heard the Word, but have not yet attained vision of it as has she. This theme of vision as higher than audition is prominent in the writings of Philo of Alexandria, which predate the redactions of the canonical Gospels. Especially in his *De migratione Abrahami*, we find passages like this:

> The sage is he who sees. Fools are blind and nearsighted. Thus prophets were called "seers" in olden times (1 Sm. 9:9). Did not the ascetic take care to exchange ear for eye, so as to see what he could only hear before? Thus he became heir to the kingdom of seeing, and went beyond that of hearing. Henceforth the coin of study and teaching evoked by the name of Jacob is stamped with the new image of Israel, the See.[107] This is the entrance of the vision of divine light, which is the same as science. And this science opens the eye of the

---

[106] 1 Jn 1:2; and Jn 8:56.

[107] *Israël* in Hebrew signifies "who sees God."

soul so as to lead it to apprehensions that are clearer and more luminous than those of the ear.[108]

It is God who makes us see; it is the Light that awakens the light
within us. Philo comes to a conclusion that is hard for many to accept:
"To see is better than to possess." He offers the example of Moses seeing
the Promised Land from afar, as told in Deuteronomy 34:4: "When He
had shown Moses the entire land, God said to him: 'I have made you see
with your eyes, but you shall not enter there.'"

Do not believe that this is any sort of stricture upon this greatest of
sages, as some narrow minds have maintained. No, what this is telling us
is that the prerogatives of adults are not to be confused with those of children. The latter are called exercise, the former wisdom. It follows that the
wonders of nature are meant more to be seen than possessed (*possedere*
meaning "to sit upon"). Is possession still possible for one who participates
greatly in the Divine? But vision remains possible for such a one. Though
such vision is not given to everyone, it is at least possible for the most
purified people, whose vision has been honed, and to whom the Father of
the Universe has shown his own works.

What life can surpass the life of contemplation? What could be more
fitting for a being endowed with reason? It is because of this that,
although the voice of mortals is meant for the ear, the word of God, like
light, is meant to be seen. It is written that "All the people saw the
voice"[109] instead of "heard the voice," because there was in fact no shak-
ing of the air from any organs of mouth or tongue. This was the splendor
of virtue, the very source of the Logos.[110]

Yet the Deuteronomist tradition seems opposed to this primacy of

---

[108]Philo of Alexandria, *De migratione Abrahami* (Editions du Cerf, 1965), 109. See also *De confusione linguarum*, 140–48; and *De Abrahamo*, 150. In English, see his collected works in *Philo*, Colson and Whitaker, trans., Loeb Classical Library (Cambridge, Mass.: , Harvard Univiversity Press, 1962).

[109][This is in fact the more literally correct translation of Ex 20:18, though not the usual one. Chouraqui agrees, but has "voices" instead of "voice."—*Trans.*]

[110]*De migratione Abrahami*, p. 123.

vision over audition. Nevertheless, a thorough examination of Hebrew literature shows that these two organs of perception are meant to complement, not to oppose one another. On the one hand, it is said that the ear must be primary, for "man cannot see God and live."[111] On the other hand, it is also supposed to be possible to see and contemplate God: "Moses went up, along with Aaron, Hadab, Abihu, and seventy of the elders of Israel. They saw the God of Israel. . . . They contemplated God, and then ate and drank."[112]

This ancient debate was taken up yet again by the Fathers of the Roman Church.[113] But all the polemics in favor of one sense or the other tend to pale when we remember that it is not our physical, outer senses that are called upon, but our inner ones—sometimes called the eye of the heart or the innermost ear.

Even Philo spoke of intuition in this sense: "It is said that God 'saw' all that he had made, but this does not mean that he directed his eyes to these realities, but that he had the intuition, knowledge, and apprehension of what he had made."[114]

So the question posed by the Gospel of Mary is not whether those who hear the Teacher or see him are more privileged. The question is how this inner audition (for Peter) and this inner vision, the eye of the nous (for Miriam), are possible. This requires that we take into consideration the context of anthropological beliefs surrounding this gospel—and let us recall that the very existence of this Coptic version suggests that we are dealing with an anthropology that cannot be encompassed by Greek and Semitic worldviews.

Miriam's declaration is forthright and candid:

"I had a vision of the Teacher . . ."[115]

---

[111]Among others, see Ex 33:20; Jgs 6:22–23; Is 6:5.

[112]Ex 24:9–11.

[113]See Clement of Alexandria, *Stromates* VI, 3.34, 1–3; and Origen VI, Celsius 62.

[114]*De migratione Abrahami*, 121.

[115]Cf. Jn 20:18, where she says to the disciples: "I have seen the Lord!" prior to relating his words to her.

She is not troubled or agitated by this vision, which again is a sign of the inner peace that governs her emotional and psychic powers. This vision is neither a dream, a fantasy, a trance, nor one of those cataleptic states brought about by techniques current in those times (in those days there were numerous schools of prophecy, not unlike our contemporary schools of channeling or mediumship).

Miriam remains undisturbed, and like Theresa of Avila and other later visionaries, she speaks directly to the Teacher:

> *"Lord, I see you now*
> *in this vision."*

She *addresses* what she sees, and what she sees *addresses* her. Thus there is no opposition of word and vision. Just as he did in his mortal existence, the Teacher responds to Miriam's thirst for truth and knowledge:

> *"You are blessed, for the sight of me does not disturb you."*

From the beginning, she possesses this grace of not being caught up in psychic excitation when confronted with this phenomenon—which could also be seen as freedom from the dualism of visible vs. invisible, or material vs. spiritual Reality. She remains in the same intimacy with him as when he lived in space-time. Having gone beyond space-time, he is just as alive, and it is this to which she bears witness:

> *"There where is the nous, lies the treasure."*

These exact words have often been quoted in later Christian writings, such as those of Clement of Alexandria, Justin, Macarios and a number of others, which is evidence that the Gospel of Mary circulated widely during the first centuries of Christianity. It is important to remember that nous has no such place in the Gospels of Luke and Matthew, which substitute the word *heart* and change the tense from present to future: For where your treasure is, there your heart will be also.[116]

The usual meaning of *kardia* is the "general inner nature of a person." To speak of nous rather than of kardia has far deeper significance than merely a stylistic difference. We could even say that it suggests something specific about what Yeshua's anthropology might have been. Especially in the passages that follow this one, the Gospel of Mary displays a kind of revealed anthropology. Of course this is bound to be of interest to us, given all the current difficulties and confusions in this domain.

As Anne Pasquier points out, this passage from the Gospel of Mary is certainly related to the teaching of the Presence of the Son of Man within every human being. Hence the treasure referred to in these lines is not some pie-in-the-sky, nor is it of some future time.

In the Gospel of Mary, the nous does not represent the whole human being, nor even an element, such as heart or intellect, which will someday have to discover the treasure. For here there is no more division between the treasure that one must acquire little by little, and oneself. There is no difference between the treasure and that part of us that is the nous—the nous is the treasure, an inner element that the disciple has no need to acquire through some moral action, but something that he already possesses by nature, and that must also be discovered.

Furthermore, the absence of the possessive pronoun in the Gospel of Mary indicates that the nous represents far more than the individual or personal soul:

> *"There where is the nous, lies the treasure."*[117]

In other words, we become what we love and we become what we know. My desire for Being is Being itself, desiring itself in me. As Meister Eckhart said, "The eye with which I see God is the eye with which he sees me."

---

[116]Lk 12:34; Mt 6:21—*Opou gar estin o thesauros umón ekei kai è kardia umón estaï.*
[117]Pasquier, *L'Evangile de Marie,* 73.

[Page 10, continued]

17   *"Then I said to him:*

18   *'Lord, when someone meets you*

19   *in a Moment of vision,*

20   *is it through the soul [psyche] that they see,*

21   *or is it through the Spirit [Pneuma] ?'*

22   *The Teacher answered:*

23   *'It is neither through the soul nor the spirit,*

24   *but the nous between the two*

25   *which sees the vision, and it is this which . . .'"*

[Pages 11–14 are missing]

The canonical Gospels, even that of John, have left us unprepared for this kind of question. It is as if the disciples of those gospels were totally uninterested in epistemological or metaphysical questions. Being men of practical intelligence, they were concerned only with questions of how to live and act. It is as if they had no interest in probing the nature of their own knowledge and perception of the resurrected Christ. But what is the basis of belief in their perception of the resurrected Christ ? Is there a way of knowing real vision from vision that merely seems to be real? And how does this gnosis work—what are its means and organs of perception? Such questions are not asked, and it would seem that you have either to believe it or not.

Are these a woman's questions? Or questions of a man endowed with intuitive and imaginative intelligence? In any case, Miriam of Magdala's questions are important ones, for the question of how one *knows* the resurrected Christ is also a question of the nature of Reality itself and involves the very foundations of Christianity.

But isn't all this just a representation—a story that has been experienced, thought, dreamed, imagined, told, and retold? If so, how does such a representation originate? Is the story fiction or truth? In the very asking of this question, we see how invested we are in a certain Western mode of thought and interpretation: the either/or assumption—either it's a dream, or else it's real. Any third possibility is excluded.

And what if it is precisely in this excluded third possibility that Reality lies: a kind of synthesis or reunion of subject and object that had temporarily been dissociated so as to make the representation intelligible? And how is all of this possible? How is a representation of the resurrected Christ possible? How did Christianity become possible?

We can begin to understand why some disciples were taken aback by the audacity of such a question:

> *"'Lord, when someone meets you*
> *in a Moment of vision,*
> *is it through the soul [psyche] that they see,*
> *or is it through the Spirit [Pneuma]?'"*

In other words, how is it possible that I see you, and through what eyes? Are they the eyes of the psyche, or of the spirit? Many people today would reduce this to, "Am I going crazy, or am I a mystic?" Still others couldn't care less about the distinction between psychic and spiritual experience, for both belong to psychopathology, and people who see such things probably need help. They are in the same class as others who have hallucinations of things that are not of this world—the world that everybody sees with the eyes of consensus. After all, what other world is there? This view, which is still very influential, would have us deny the existence of a different perception or consensus than the dominant one.

The Teacher's answer does not make things easy for us, especially considering the unfortunate lack of pages 11–14. It would seem that he is just about to develop this theme and perhaps even reveal his anthropology of different modes of knowledge.

But this could also be seen as a blessing in disguise. It certainly encourages our humility as exegetes—there will always be a huge question mark in our interpretations, and this gap may offer a space of freedom for those who want to take their quest further. Thus we continue to feel the

lack of any adequate, tangible representation of the Real that can be imagined or thought. And the yearning for Truth with which this leaves us is
in fact the source of our aliveness:

> *"The Teacher answered:*
> *'It is neither through the soul nor the spirit,*
> *but the nous between the two*
> *which sees the vision, and it is this which . . .'"*

These fragments give rise to a number of reflections: First, this apparition of the resurrected Christ to Miriam is of neither a purely psychic nor
a purely spiritual order. The language of Roman Catholicism from the era
of Gardeil, Lubac, Maritain, and so forth, would interpret this as being
"neither natural nor supernatural." However, the response in this gospel
compels us to go beyond this binary mode of thinking in which our brain
normally operates. The excluded middle of our dualism is:

> *"'. . . the nous between the two*
> *which sees the vision, and it is this which . . .'"*

It is up to us to complete the ellipsis. This would of course be influenced by our anthropological beliefs—but it would be better if we were to
use our own imaginal capacity. The possibilities are endless, of course . . .
but is each of them Real? Which of them are necessary and true? Which
are most in harmony with the silence that permeates this discontinuity in
the sayings of Yeshua?

It is the nous that . . . sees? Feels? Intuits? Imagines? Knows? Loves?
Is aware?[118] The choice is ours, provided that we are very clear as to what
we mean by seeing, hearing, imagining, knowing, loving.

Before making a choice, let us outline several systems of anthropology

---

[118][The psyche normally performs these functions, but here the nous uses the psyche to perform them
on a higher level, permeated with spirit.—*Trans.*]

in which the place of nous may be considered, in the light of its importance in the Gospel of Mary.

1. There is no place for it in any modern one-dimensional anthropology, where a human being is regarded as being essentially a physical body, however complex—a mere composite form that will soon decompose and be no more. There is not even adequate space for psyche here, much less for spirit (nous). Intelligence is reduced to a play of energy in neural networks, a phenomenon of the brain. Certainly there is no place for an entity such as the Holy Spirit (Pneuma)—all such notions are mere comforting illusions to cushion us from the certainty of the annihilation of death.

2. It also has no place in a dualistic anthropology of body/mind split, such as the Cartesian worldview. Such an anthropology ignores the nous and the Pneuma. Although there is some place for psychic, or soul activity, there is neither spirit nor Spirit.[119]

3. It does have a place in Platonic and Neoplatonic systems. Human beings have a body, a soul, and a spirit: soma, psyche, and nous. The spirit is the divine dimension, which needs to be liberated from the clutches of sensations (soma) and emotions (psyche).

4. In the Gospel of Mary, however, the nous is not presented as the fully Divine in us, but as the intermediary between the realm of psyche (soul) and the realm of Pneuma (Spirit). It is the Pneuma—the Breath, or Holy Spirit—that is considered as truly divine in the anthropology of this gospel. This brings us to a fourfold anthropology in which the nous also finds its rightful place, though it is a different one from that in the Platonic system. Thus the human being is a composite of body (soma), soul (psyche), mind (nous), and Spirit (Pneuma).

This Pneuma is not itself a component of the human complex, however, but the Reality that gives life to the other components. In this

---

[119][The word *spirit* or *mind* is often used in Cartesian-type philosophies, but there is no distinction between higher and lower mind, or between spirit and soul. Everything non-physical is reduced to the same psychic level.—*Trans.*]

perspective, to become spiritual is not to disincarnate (i.e., to arise from the tomb of the body), nor is it to deny our feelings and emotions (i.e., psychic activity and the happy/unhappy memories that underlie it). It does not imply any devaluing of the *mind* aspect of the noetic dimension of humanness, which includes intellect, intuition, and imagination—an intelligence capable of forming ideas or representations (images) of the Real. Instead, spiritualization is a process of imbuing these different dimensions of the human being with the presence of the Holy Spirit, or Pneuma. This transfigures the body, expands and calms the soul, and it simplifies and clarifies the mind and spirit (nous). Here is a summary of these for view:

1 — One-Dimensional Humanity
One material body, intelligent and impermanent
The body is the only value. There is no reality beyond that of its space-time.

2 — Two-Dimensional Humanity
— soul (psyche) immortal
— body (soma), mortal
The body is animated by an informative value that is perhaps non-mortal and independent of the body's space-time (which is not the same as eternal, inasmuch as the latter is defined as beyond all possible space-times).

3 — Three-Dimensional Humanity
— spirit (nous)
— soul (psyche)
— body (soma)
The psychosomatic complex is joined to a spirit (nous) that is considered as the supreme value.

4 — Fourfold Humanity
Spirit (Pneuma)
— spirit, (nous)
— soul (psyche)
— body (soma)

The human complex (body, soul, spirit) has an opening through its spirit or higher mind (nous) to a dimension beyond space-time, known as the Pneuma or Holy Spirit.

It is this last, fourfold anthropology that is probably that of the Gospel of Mary. It embraces both the Platonic and Neoplatonic Greek traditions (body-soul-spirit) as well as the Semitic tradition, which equates the Pneuma with the Hebrew *ruah*, the Holy Breath or Holy Spirit that gives the human complex its life and coherence.

There are various ways of symbolizing this anthropology (see figure 4):

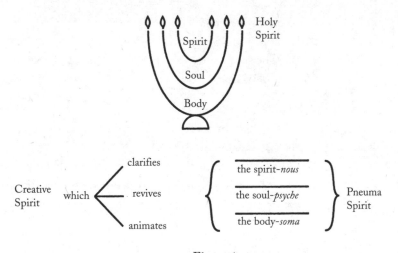

Figure 4

According to the Gospel of Mary, it is precisely this nous (human higher mind or spirit) that receives the Pneuma (Spirit of God) and transmits its fire and light to the other elements of the human complex.

If we apply this anthropology to our previous figure of Anthropos, while trying to avoid over complexity, then we might arrive at the scheme in figure 5. [Note: Words in roman in figure 5 refer to figure 4, which represents the human being in its process of becoming; words in italics in figure 5 refer to the underlying anthropology deduced from the passage 10:17–25 of the Gospel of Mary.—*Trans.*]

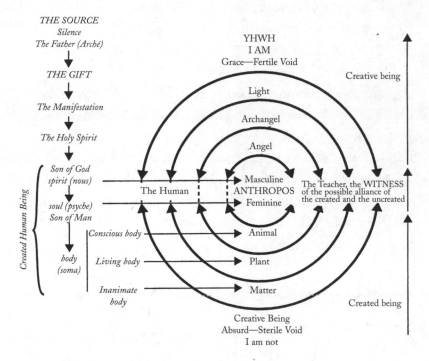

Figure 5

In both figures 4 and 5, the most important region is the junction—the relation, or bridge—between two different realms of Being. Many aspects of this bridge are shown, the ultimate of which is that of the unthinkable and inconceivable alliance of Being and nonbeing; of the I AM and the I am not.

Various elements of these systems are also to be found later in the writings of the early Church Fathers, especially in the anthropological synthesis of the Christian tradition by Maximus the Confessor.

> The sinner—meaning the unhappy, unbalanced human being—
> is one who is cut off from the Holy Spirit.
> The human spirit (nous), having turned away from the Spirit of
> God, the Pneuma, now turns toward its own soul (psyche), and
> this entangles it in the passions (*pathé*, or "pathologies").

The soul then turns toward the body (soma) and becomes a slave
of its sensations and instincts.

The body, having nothing toward which to turn, returns to nothingness.

All that is composed is decomposed.

The *theos-anthropos* undertaking would seem to have failed.

The happy (well-balanced, "normal," "saved") human being is one
whose spirit or mind (nous) is turned toward the Pneuma and looks and
listens for the messages communicated by the Breath. Such a mind is able
to orient and clarify the psyche. The psyche then transmits its light to the
body, bringing it vitality and peace.

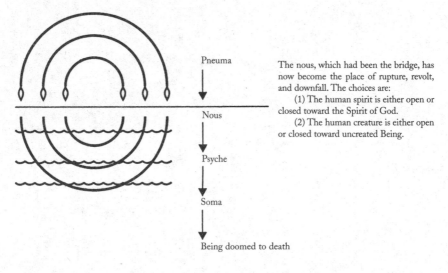

The nous, which had been the bridge, has
now become the place of rupture, revolt,
and downfall. The choices are:
    (1) The human spirit is either open or
closed toward the Spirit of God.
    (2) The human creature is either open
or closed toward uncreated Being.

Figure 6

This is the human being who is completely turned toward the divine
or uncreated Being. This is the human who becomes Anthropos, the
union of theos and anthropos. Such individuals are able to freely appropriate all of the potentials written in their genetic heritage, plus those
granted by the opening of their humanity (see figure 7).

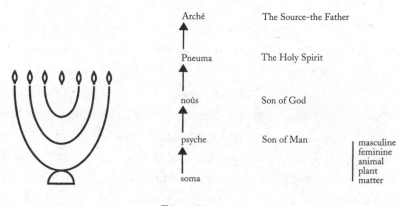

Figure 7

Yet much remains to be said about the specific nature of this nous, which is neither completely psychic, nor completely spiritual, and which forms the bridge between two.

> "'... the nous between the two
> which sees the vision, and it is this which ...'"

Might we complete this sentence with " . . . sees and hears"? It would at least bring together the partisans of vision and audition, Greek and Semite alike. But if we stick to the text as we have it, the focus is on vision, and it is through the nous that one sees. For Miriam, the apparition of the resurrected One thus becomes not just a belief or a possibility, but a certainty and reality.

We could even go so far as to say that it is the very foundations of Christianity that are at stake, inasmuch as these embrace the love and knowledge of the Christ who was witnessed to have lived, taught, and suffered, and who was crucified, killed, and buried, and who was witnessed after his death as resurrected and alive, and who is still present now—who, according to his words in Matthew 28:20, is "with you always, unto the end of the age."

This suggests several hypotheses regarding the nature of "that which sees," and which seems to see through the mind or imagination. This especially evokes an experience very similar to that explored by Henry Corbin in his numerous works on mystics and saints, which he calls the creative imagination (following Ibn Arabi), or the imaginal.

But we might also consider what has been said by some thinkers less open to charges of mysticism than Corbin. For example, in the *Critique of Pure Reason*, Kant has some interesting things to say regarding the place and specific limits of the imagination, which he considers to be the faculty of synthesis: "I mean synthesis in the most general sense of the word: the act of adding together diverse representations so as to comprehend this diversity in knowledge."

Thus addition becomes unification. Kant continues:

> Synthesis in general is [. . .] the simple effect of the imagination, that is to say, of a human faculty that is blind but indispensible, and without which we could never have any sort of knowledge, though we are only very rarely aware of this.

Christian Jambet comments on this text:

> It is clear that the "blind" imagination is for us dark, hidden, and mute, for it does not reveal anything in particular to us, and especially nothing imaginary. It gives nothing more than the world, and just the world. Its place is close to the ultimate root of subjectivity: transcendental apperception, which unifies the totality of the given and the edifice of judgments. This place is so enigmatic that Heidegger, meditating upon the most famous passages of the *Critique*, coined this most striking résumé: "The transcendental imagination is without a homeland." [120]

Returning to texts that are more akin to the Gospel of Mary, we

---

[120]Jambet, *La Logique des Orientaux*, p. 60.

might recall the words of Yeshua to the Pharisees, reminding them that it is those who claim that they see who are the most blind, and that: "I came into this world so that those who are blind might see. . . ."[121]

The nous—or creative imagination—of Miriam is in a sense blind, and this is paradoxically why she is able to see. As Heidegger said, her imagination is "without a homeland." In other words, it is without a ground, without matter to be seen, without a body that can be touched. And yet she sees. She sees the One who animates and forms this body and this matter that she had previously been able to perceive only through the physical senses. She has passed into another mode of knowing, where Yeshua tells her (in Jn 20:17) not to detain him through touch, that is not to try to reduce him to sensible and conceptual categories of the known.

The philosopher Berkeley, like Malebranche, maintained that ideas are not private phenomena pertaining to an individual, but independent, non-material entities quite distinct from the soul and its modifications.[122] For Berkeley, as for the great Iranian mystics Suhrawardi and Mullah Sadra Shirazi, there is the same paradox of sensation: Although the imaginal is a modification of the soul, it is presentational knowledge rather than a representational knowledge. It is a presentational knowledge (*hoduri,* in Persian) where the reality is the image itself. The imaginal is not just an individual way of functioning, but an independent entity.

Surely it is among such authors as these that we must search, reflect, and meditate if we are to come closer to the reality contemplated by Miriam of Magdala, a reality that is neither the fruit of her projections, nor of some need to be filled with what remains of Yeshua in her memory. This reality is not objective in the same sense that the term is applied to ordinary reality, for this resurrection is not something that can be captured so as to weigh, measure and explain it with the faculties of sensation and reason, those powers that have become so dear to us in the one-dimensional reality in which the Teacher was previously perceived.

---

[121]Jn 9:39.

[122]See George Berkeley, *Philosophical Commentaries,* George H. Thomas, ed. (Ohio: Alliance, 1976).

There are anthropologies infinitely richer than that of one-dimensional humanity. It is the latter point of view that always reduces any phenomenon of resurrection to something unreal—yet there is no evidence that history itself is one-dimensional. The Gospel of Mary's purpose is to open up our vision of humanity and its history. The blinders that we wear are ultimately our own choice and responsibility.

Yet it is also true that we cannot be too careful about interpreting the ellipses in the text,

> *"It is neither through the soul nor the spirit,*
> *but the nous between the two*
> *which sees the vision, and it is this which . . .'"*

[Page 15]

1   *"And Craving said:*

2   *'I did not see you descend,*

3   *but now I see you rising.*

4   *Why do you lie, since you belong to me?'*

5   *The soul answered:*

6   *'I saw you,*

7   *though you did not see me,*

8   *nor recognize me.*

9   *I was with you as with a garment,*

10   *and you never felt me.'*

11   *Having said this,*

12   *the soul left, rejoicing greatly.*

In the previous chapter Miriam taught the disciples that we are able to see visions by grace of the nous.

In this vision the Resurrection is not merely an event of the past, but the imaginal, transhistorical symbol of all love that is linked with a body of flesh and blood, and that is victorious over the space-time by which it

was believed to have been limited. This Resurrection abides and continues far beyond any date and time at which it was empirically witnessed.
Its space must be both physical (otherwise it disappears from history) and
spiritual (otherwise it disappears into history). It is the nous that perceives
this zone between the purely physical and the purely spiritual worlds.

If this dimension of humanness is denied or still dormant, there is an
entire climate of Reality that remains undiscovered. Yet even beyond the
nous there is the Pneuma . . . and beyond the Pneuma, the Silence *(sigè)*.
In the Gospel of Mary, the Kingdom is also called Repose and Silence.

Visionary experience is a necessary stage between words and the
Silence—but words, vision, and silence are only particular steps in this
great voyage from matter toward light, which is also known as a human
being. Or better yet, the human being is the memory and storytelling of
this voyage. Undoubtedly we would know more about the vicissitudes of
this adventure if pages 11–14 were not missing.

Before attaining the Repose of Silence, Miriam's being must pass
through four climates,[123] the final and uppermost of which consists
of seven levels. At the opening of page 15, Miriam has already passed
through the first climate. She has left behind the experience of nausea so
well described in our contemporary literature—that sense of disgust and
absurdity at being too full of matter, trapped and stifled by the weight of
our consituent elements.

Of course we must also live with love and appreciation for our passage through materiality. But when its weight usurps all our space, when
we no longer feel in us even the faintest beating of the wings of levity, the
experience of this materiality descends not only toward a subhuman stupor, but toward an experience of "bad nothingness"; although the vehicle
is empty, it still has no room.

---

[123]Other translations have rendered this as "powers," "energies," or "authorities." I have preferred "climate." Some climates are healthy, others unhealthy. A climate is something that can surprise and
envelop us; thus it has power and authority over us. This is why people speak of psychological climates or atmospheres. In this gospel the different climates are also personified. We move through the
climates of Craving, Ignorance, and so forth, before arriving at the fair and peaceful climate of the
presence of Being.

IV. FOURTH CLIMATE
Sevenfold Wrath

Darkness, craving, ignorance, lethal jealousy, enslavement to the body, intoxicated wisdom, guileful wisdom

A climate that adds its violence to the other climates, bringing them to climaxes of jealousy, possessiveness, pride, and the madness of profane wisdom

III. THIRD CLIMATE
Refusal of Knowledge

Willful ignorance, refusal of awareness

A climate of stupor, closed-mindedness, complacency, and vanity

II. SECOND CLIMATE
Craving

The desire to possess

A tense and stressful climate of complaints and demands

I. FIRST CLIMATE
Darkness or Absurdity

The sterile void

A nauseating climate where our identification with matter engenders the experience of our nothingness and meaninglessness

Figure 8

The Gospel of Mary now recounts the soul's dialogue with Craving, a symbol of the trial that every psyche must face in crossing this second climate:

> *"And Craving said:*
> *'I did not see you descend,*
> *but now I see you rising.*
> *Why do you lie . . . ?'"*

Indeed, the soul does lie, inasmuch as it belongs to Craving. If Craving can make us rise (and toward what?), it can all the more make us fall. This is a climate of possessiveness. We have all been warned against being possessed by our possessions. As long as Craving drives us, we will never have peace. Craving can never say "Enough," only "More."

"Why do you lie, since you belong to me?"

But Craving cannot conceal its true identity as *the very nature of the psyche* alone, the nature of all psychic activity that has been cut off from spirit. The soul in this condition can never be satisfied, and it is this ever-growing demand that is bound to become more vehement, and culminate in wrath.

Yet Miriam's soul is clear, for the light of the nous lives in it, so that she is able to *see*, and to answer:

> *"I saw you,*
> *though you did not see me,*
> *nor recognize me.'"*

The soul that is illumined by nous is turned toward spiritual Reality and is open to the breath of Pneuma—it *sees* the mechanisms and convolutions of psychic activity; but the soul, when left to itself, cannot see these. This highlights the problematic aspect of many so-called psychics who claim to be in contact with spiritual realities. An authentically spiritual person is capable of understanding a person driven by craving and possessiveness. But a person who is merely psychic cannot understand a spiritual person, one who is guided by non-attachment and is capable of free and unselfish acts. The psychic always has a tendency to reduce the acts of the spiritual person to its own limited categories—for example, labeling the behavior of the latter as hypocritical, incomprehensible, or deluded.

"I was with you as with a garment,[124]
and you never felt me.'"

Craving *(epithumia)* is like a garment for the soul. It is a robe richly colored with bright and dark places, no doubt, but it is not an essential manifestation of the soul, nor even of its physical envelope, the body. The soul could instead put on a garment of generosity or kindness, or of any of a number of other animate forms. The very nature of Craving is inflation—pretending to be something it is not. In this case, it has taken itself for the envelope or skin of the soul, rather than as a mere costume. But it cannot truly feel.

"Having said this,
the soul left, rejoicing greatly."

Having affirmed its freedom from its clothing—its forms—the soul can leave in joy. Miriam's own psychic activity thus shows that it is not alienated through identification with its cravings. This is akin to its previous liberation from identification with its nausea or aversion.

Is not the psyche that has passed through the climates of attraction and repulsion already on the path of nous and Pneuma? Is it not already able to taste a fully spiritual joy or, in other words, a joy that is not the mere result of success in avoiding pain or attaining pleasure, but a simple rejoicing in *that which is*, regardless of whether it is agreeable or disagreeable? This is the gift that is granted to the soul so that it may continue its ascent in the evolution of its consciousness.

[Page 15, continued]

13   *Then it entered into the third climate,*
14   *known as Ignorance.*

---

[124][The author's translation of this passage differs from most others. The MacRae/Wilson version, for example, has the soul say to Craving: "I served you as a garment . . ." Leloup reverses this, making Craving the garment of the soul, which would seem to make better sense.—*Trans.*]

15   *Ignorance inquired of the soul:*

16   *'Where are you going?*

17   *You are dominated by wicked inclinations.*

18   *Indeed, you lack discrimination, and you are enslaved.'*

The third climate is one of complacent or willful ignorance. We prefer not to know, for knowing would imply a conscience and responsibilities. "We didn't know," or "We were just obeying orders," have now become familiar excuses given by those judged for crimes against humanity. We would in fact prefer not to really know that our enemy is *also* a human being, and thus a brother or sister, in spite of apparent differences such as race or culture.

This refusal of awareness, this lethargy that blocks certain incoming knowledge, is ultimately capable of making us accomplices in the most atrocious crimes. Yet this ignorance brings no peace to the soul, and those who have it are not as blissful as they might appear. A questioning must sooner or later come to shake them out of it: Where are you going? What is your path and what is the meaning of your life?

Awareness of our own ignorance can be our salvation. Does not wisdom begin with consciousness of our own not-knowing, just as healing begins with consciousness of our own lack of health?

"'You are dominated by wicked inclinations.'"

What is it that "inclines" us to do this or that? What is it that makes us lean toward one attitude instead of another? As André Gide said, "Yes, you do have to go with the slope—but upwards!"

It is right and useful to explore and to know our own inclinations—all our attractions and repulsions—so as not to become reduced to being their unconscious slaves. Thus the accusations would seem to apply to a soul that is unable to resist its inclinations:

"'Indeed, you lack discrimination,[125] *and you are enslaved.'"*

What is lacking in such a soul is that *diacrisis*, discrimination or discernment, that enables it to resist identifying with its inclinations. We must not mistake our true nature for that which is defined by our inclinations. Of course we *have* desires, but we *are not* these desires. This confusion is another aspect of ignorance, a dreadful mixing-up of our being as subject with the objects of its desire.

Discrimination begins with separation: What I am from what I am not; and what I desire from what I do not desire. Of course these things are not always so clear. Unfortunately, this human limitation often becomes used as an excuse to defend our ignorance; we can claim that we are all just mixtures after all—especially of consciousness and unconsciousness.

The climate of willful ignorance is strangely perpetuated by all sorts of pseudo-understandings like this. They offer us a cheap and clever escape from guilt, which only makes us behave more and more irresponsibly. We cannot truly become free of guilt if we try to escape the grain of consciousness implicit in it. It is precisely this consciousness that enables us to *discern* our bad inclinations. This does not mean judging or condemning them, or feeling guilty about them—it means knowing them well enough so that we do not become easy prey for them.

The passage from animal to human requires discrimination, the capacity to evaluate and judge one's acts favorably or unfavorably. Chimpanzees can create works of art with their agile hands, occasionally achieving quite remarkable paintings in color. But it is useless to look for even a hint of discrimination or evaluation on the part of the chimps.[126] The anthropology of the Gospel of Mary reminds us that a multitude of talented monkeys cannot accomplish what one creature of discrimination

---

[125]From the Indo-European root *skeri*, which means "to cut," "divide," common with Greek *krinein*, which means "to discern," "discriminate," "separate, " "judge."

[126]Based on laboratory experiments conducted by the author with "painter" chimpanzees at UCLA in 1980.

can do. Is not the world of human society in reality a jungle—or rather a circus—where talented monkeys reign supreme?

The willfully ignorant are wont to follow this inclination that leads back to the animal they were but can no longer be, because it allows escape from the trials of self-knowledge and the demands of discrimination. Not wanting to know is the most powerful and destructive of forces, ultimately resulting in that self-indulgent cowardice that alone makes it possible for people to allow and participate in all the injustices and crimes of the world.

Just as ignorance of the law is no excuse for committing a crime, so is choosing to be unaware of another's suffering no excuse for inaction, for it is a willful ignorance that can only exacerbate our stupor of cowardice and irresponsibility as long as it continues.

Here the Gospel of Mary is closest to the traditions of India, which teach that the root of all evil is ignorance. It is ignorance that enslaves us and makes us indifferent, and indifference is the wretched climate surrounding all comfortably numbed consciences.

> **[Page 15, continued]**
> 19   *The soul answered:*
> 20   *'Why do you judge me, since I have made no judgment?*
> 21   *I have been dominated, but I myself have not dominated.*
> 22   *I have not been recognized,*
> 23   *but I myself have recognized*
> 24   *that all things which are composed shall be decomposed,*
> 25   *on earth and in heaven.'"*

The human psyche has always been adept at finding excuses. "She made me do it, God," as Adam said. It can use virtually anything, invoking God, the Devil, childhood trauma, genes, or destiny. What is the source of this frantic need to believe oneself innocent? It is not as if the only alternative to this were some threat of a guilt-ridden, masochistic conscience. The alternative is simply a bit more lucidity, courage, and awareness—knowledge of our ability to respond and our responsibility for our acts, words, desires, and life. But even a little more lucidity seems to be too much to bear for a petty ego swollen by a psyche teeming with memories.

> *"The soul answered:*
> *'Why do you judge me, since I have made no judgment?'"*

It is true that the soul, or psyche, cannot discriminate by itself. It is only by virtue of the nous acting within the soul that discrimination is possible, for only through the nous can the soul receive the vision of what is and what is not.[127] The unregenerate soul has forgotten that it has only to turn toward the light of the nous in order to have access to a different climate where innocence means, instead of ignorance, wholeness and harmony of actions and words and of knowledge and being, even though our knowledge is always partial, and our realization of being is never perfect.

> *"I have been dominated, but I myself have not dominated."*

Here the psyche recognizes how it has been dominated by circumstances, events, environment, and conditioning. It sees how it has been more the plaything than the player in the events of its life. Stating that "I myself have not dominated" is a recognition that we have not been in control of the game.

This reveals the profoundly passive disposition of the soul—a sublime disposition when it orients itself to the higher power coming through the nous, but an unhealthy passivity when "I myself have not dominated"

---

[127]This is why Yeshua, who embodies the nous that is turned toward the Pneuma, and who incarnates the Anthropos, or fully *human* being, is able to say (in Jn 12:44–48): "He who believes in me, believes not in me but in him who sent me. And he who sees me sees him who sent me. I have come as light into the world, that whoever believes in me may not remain in darkness. If any one hears my sayings and does not keep them, I do not judge him; for I did not come to judge the world but to save the world. He who rejects me and does not receive my sayings has a judge; the word that I have spoken will be his judge on the last day."

becomes an escape or an attempt to excuse one's complacency with "At least *I* haven't done any harm—I was just the victim of circumstances." This can only lead the psyche downward to ever-flimsier rationalizations and ever-baser instincts.

And yet:

> *"I have not been recognized,*
> *but I myself have recognized*
> *that all things which are composed shall be decomposed,*
> *on earth and in heaven.'"*

Here is revealed that flash of lucidity, that spark of nous that some mystics have called the finest point of the soul. This is knowledge of emptiness, and of the vanity of all things in time. Nothing escapes the metaphysical lightning-flash of such a soul.

Everything on earth and in heaven is of the created realm, and therefore impermanent, with no being in itself. As the Latin version of the opening of the Gospel of John says, *Sine ipsum, nihil*. Without the Creator, nothing. Without the information of the creative Logos, nothing can truly exist. In the very core of its alienation and false identities, in the darkest heart of the stupor that typifies this climate of ignorance, the psyche has the possibility of *seeing* its own sheer nothingness. This paradoxical evidence, this total disillusionment, is also the beginning of liberation, for it is the doorway to selfless love, unattached to illusions. It is this love that will strengthen the soul so that it will be able to deal with its own turbulence in the fourth climate, which is an intensified recapitulation of all its previous trials.

[Page 16]

1   *"Freed from this third climate, the soul continued its*
     ascent,

2   *and found itself in the fourth climate.*

3   *This has seven manifestations:*

4   *the first manifestation is Darkness;*

5   *the second, Craving;*

6   *the third, Ignorance;*

7   *the fourth, Lethal Jealousy;*

The psyche's insight into its own nothingness has enabled it to leave the third climate of Ignorance, where it risked falling into unconsciousness. But curiously, the next trial awaiting it after this insight is not some mood of despair or horror, as one might suppose from the symbol of darkness. Instead, the soul travels henceforth into an atmosphere of ever-increasing wrath and rebellion.

According to some modern psychologies—which recognize no higher dimensions of the kind exemplified by nous and Pneuma—anger is a completely logical and normal reaction to being confronted with one's own powerlessness; and being nothing is of course unacceptable to a psyche whose desire is to be something at any price.

This anger is like that of a child faced with its own inability to lift a weight that an adult finds easy to handle. If the child can accept being simply a child, there will be no anger.[128] Likewise, if psychic activity can accept being simply psychic activity, and if a creature can accept being simply a creature, no problem of wrath or revolt will arise. But when the psyche does not accept the limits of its own activity, it becomes like the child who wants to be an adult or the creature who fancies itself in the place of the Creator. The soul is engulfed in a climate of demand, complaint, agitation, and violence, a caricature of authentic action and a cacophony of war drums for a meaningless spectacle.

The soul generates sound and fury so as to maintain its illusion of existence, but it is like scratching at a violin and calling it music. This illusory existence is accompanied and fed by manifestations that are known all too well. The soul, dwelling in ever-darker shadows, may take perverse pleasure at cursing a God whom it holds responsible for its misery, and

---

[128]Admiration may take the place of anger when the child loves the adult and does not seek to appear to be as strong as the latter.

mires itself in all sorts of attachment and envy. It is forever tallying its inventory of fancied needs and deprivations of being. And since these become far more important to the soul than what it already has and truly is, it becomes more complacent in its ignorance, rather than making a minimal effort to study and inquire so as to discover some understanding and meaning in its life.

We have previously encountered the first three manifestations of wrath, analyzing them as climates where the soul of Miriam risked getting lost. But they also resemble the demons mentioned in the canonical Gospels, from which she is delivered by the Teacher's love.

The fourth climate, containing seven levels, we will call Wrath. This was considered by some ancient traditions to be the worst of all demons, because of its power to thoroughly alienate the soul, which can then no longer own or recognize itself. The soul is no longer accessible—it is *possessed*, in the true sense of the term.

After someone experiences a fit of anger, we often hear him or her say things like, "I don't know what came over me," "I didn't realize what I was doing . . . I wasn't myself," or "It was as if I were possessed."

Possession is a word that applies especially well to the fourth level of this fourth climate: Jealousy. The Gospel of Mary uses a term even more specific: Lethal Jealousy. But isn't all jealousy ultimately lethal? And what of that jealousy attributed to God himself? Indeed, it is connected with his wrath, as can be seen in this passage from Deuteronomy:

> *You shall not follow other gods [. . .]*
> *For your God YHWH is a jealous*[129] *God inside you.*
> *Beware lest the wrath of YHWH your God be inflamed against you,*
> *and exterminate you from the face of the earth.*

---

[129]Dt 6:14–15.

    [André Chouraqui's literal translation of this passage from the Hebrew uses the word *ardent* instead of *jealous*: "Yes, YHWH your Elohim is an ardent El in your breast, so beware lest the nostril of YHWH be inflamed against you and exterminate you from the face of the earth."—*Trans.*]

We may recall that the doctrines of certain Gnostic sects do not consider this wrathful Old Testament deity to be the true God, but rather a malevolent demiurge, the demonic creator of a corrupted world. He is the Evil Spirit of all the bad climates that excite emotions such as jealousy and anger.

Is the god who speaks in Deuteronomy really the same God who tells Moses I AM THAT I AM? Or is it really Satan, the obstruction to Being, who is the jealous and wrathful one? It actually matters little for our purposes here. In either case, we are dealing with an outward projection of subjective psychic energies onto the cosmos and a certain tendency toward objectification and materialization.

The projection of jealousy and wrath onto God can also be interpreted as a more advanced stage of psychic evolution than it might seem. In such projections the soul is in some sense able to recognize the presence of Being in those manifestations that it fears. It discerns light in the darkness, strength in anger, and love in jealousy.

If we recognize no positive aspect whatsoever in such negative manifestations of Being, we risk even greater alienation. Evil is totally separate from good, and therefore unredeemable. This returns us to a dualistic perspective that sets up the forces of darkness against the forces of light. Evil is given more than its due, becoming a power equal to that of God. But this dualism of the good God and the evil demiurge is something that the soul is striving to overcome in its voyage.

In biblical thought the jealousy of YHWH is sometimes interpreted as a manifestation of his love, inasmuch as one imagines him to be like a father or mother who is jealous of the well-being of his or her children—like parents who cannot bear to stand by idly and watch their children lose themselves in deluded acts and ways of living that are bound to make them unhappy.

In fact, this is spelled out in the very next passage of Deuteronomy:

You shall keep the commandments of YHWH your God,
his instructions and the laws that he has prescribed for you,

and you shall do what is good and just in the eyes of YHWH
so that you may be happy [. . .][130]

YHWH becomes jealous when humans seek peace and fulfillment along paths where they are sure not to find it and through illusions that they take to be reality. Though they may experience many pleasures and comforts on these paths, they will not find authentic happiness, which can only be based on a loving and faithful relationship with Being. Thus disillusionment and suffering are inevitable.

The wrath of God can thus be seen as a symbol of a kind of immanent justice, or, as the Teacher tells us, "the result of your actions."[131] We can see this at work in all kinds of events, from the banal to the historic— from the wrath inherent in alcoholism that results in cirrhosis and the wrath of a crooked businessman leading him to prison, to the wrath in a society or culture resulting in an atmosphere of violence and war and our vast collective folly and unconsciousness that results in all kinds of earthly and heavenly consequences.

Seen in this light, certain writers years ago were justified in referring to Chernobyl as the wrath of God. Perhaps the proverb "We reap what we sow" might at times mean that we get the kind of God we deserve.

If we look, surely we can find something valuable to learn from such climates of wrath and jealousy. If, while we still have time, we are able to discern the pattern of causes and effects that have brought us into this climate, we can gain the insight that reveals actions toward our salvation, or at least our greater health and well-being.

But the Gospel of Mary does not really address a cosmic jealousy or wrath resulting from the unrecognized goodness of Being—rather, it speaks of a psychic climate of lethal jealousy that consists of the desire for *exclusive possession* of that to which we are attached, whether it be a child, a lover, or a piece of property.

---

[130]Dt 6:17–18.
[131]See above, Gospel of Mary 8:26.

We are attached to a reality that we fundamentally refuse to share. And if we are unlucky enough to have this reality escape from us, wrath is never far away. Sooner or later it will compel us to lash out, either at someone else or at ourselves. Whatever we may pretend, we fundamentally feel what we have lost to be our rightful, permanent, and inalienable possession.

Entering into authentic relation with what is dear to us and feeling and expressing such a deep-rooted refusal to share amount to a truly lethal attachment—one that finally kills off every form of relationship other than possessor and possessed.

Feeling jealousy in personal relationships always reduces others to objects—to things rather than other human beings. It excludes the possibility of meeting another as a free subject who may meet and share with still more people without losing anything of the intimacy that is unique to the dyad. The real meaning of a vow of fidelity is not intended to lead to dependence and/or alienation, but to affirm that one is capable of a fidelity that both allows and supports the complete fulfillment of another's freedom. During the ritual of marriage in the Orthodox Church, each person crowns the other. Each of the two participants never places any sort of cord around the other's neck, and the wedding ring is a symbol of alliance,[132] never of bondage.

There can be true alliance only between natures that are free and that recognize this freedom in each other through their life and behavior together. Such maturity and sovereignty are rare, because they can be achieved only by those who have been liberated from the climate of lethal jealousy that, as the enemy of mutual trust, poisons all human relationships. When trust between two beings begins to erode, it is not only jealousy and wrath that begin to take its place, it is also death.[133]

Jealousy is fundamentally murderous in the sense that it is incapable of respect and recognition of the living Anthropos in another. It ultimately reduces both others and ourselves to the level of mere matter, our

---

[132][In French the word for wedding ring is *alliance*. —*Trans.*]

[133]Cf. Wisdom 2:24: "Through the jealousy of the devil, death entered into the world."

lives to only a momentary volcanic eruption that leaves behind nothing but dead ashes and sadness.

This being said, we must not forget that, as suggested by the symbol of the jealousy of YHWH, there is another possible meaning for wrath. In certain exceptional contexts human beings are capable of manifesting what is called righteous anger, as exemplified by the Teacher driving the money changers out of the temple: "You shall not make my Father's house into a marketplace!"[134]

Yeshua is thus jealous of this space consecrated to peace and prayer, for those who use this temple have a responsibility to protect it from inner and outer influences that would debase it. His wrath is essentially directed against the calculating aspect of our mind that makes us restless and prevents us from savoring a moment of surrender, a moment of complete faith in what Life has in store for us, in spite of all our doubts and trials—a moment that is like a sweet and refreshing oasis in the midst of the most hostile climate.

For Miriam of Magdala, this oasis has both a name and a face. The memory of this Logos and the evocation of its face gives a spring to her step, even as she crosses the burning deserts of her soul.

[Page 16, continued]

8   *the fifth, Enslavement to the Body;*

9   *the sixth, Intoxicated Wisdom;*

10   *the seventh, Guileful Wisdom.*

11   *These are the seven manifestations of Wrath,*

12   *and they oppressed the soul with questions:*

13   *'Where do you come from, murderer?'*

14   *and 'Where are you going, vagabond?'*

This passage through the ordeals of different climates recalls the words of Paul to the Ephesians: "We were one of those who live according

---

[134]Jn 2:15.

to the cravings of the flesh, serving its impulses and guilty thoughts, so that our nature had become the slave of anger, just like the others."[135]

As with the canonical Gospels, we must avoid interpreting Paul's use of the word *flesh* as a synonym for the body; which is the "temple of the Spirit." Instead, it refers to the psycho-noetic human being who has become cut off from his or her spiritual roots and potential, and is reduced to mere physicality. This produces a creature who rejects any sort of amenability to a Creator, and who may appear to be self-sufficient, yet is cut off from the Source. To live within the confines of a humanity reduced to mere flesh is to live with a constant sense of powerlessness in the face of reality and death, and this again leads to the climate of wrath.

Thus the Gospel of Mary offers the same message as Paul's Letter to the Ephesians. The sixth and seventh climates come still closer to texts attributed to Paul, especially a large section of the First Letter to the Corinthians.

Before encountering the true Sophia, the Wisdom of YHWH, the Being That Is What It Is, we must also meet and unmask false wisdom. This is the wisdom called "fleshly" in the language of Paul, the wisdom whose powers are so highly esteemed in the eyes of the world. Since these powers include tremendous cunning and guile, they are able to gain widespread respect. But in reality they are inflations, forms of vanity and intoxication the very nature of which is to propel us into states of mind, or climates, where elements and powers come into play that are not our own. This is like the frog in La Fontaine's parable who thinks it can become as large as a cow by swelling—until it finally bursts.

This is the intoxication of the worldly wise who hide behind their brilliant facade of words the ruins of their ethics, the hollowness of their hearts, and the fraudulence of the very wisdom they claim to possess. For it is written in the First Letter of Paul to the Corinthians:

> "I will destroy the wisdom of the wise, and the cleverness of the clever I will thwart."

---

[135] Eph 2:3.

Where is the wise man? Where is the scribe? Where is the debater of
this age? Has not God made foolish the wisdom of the world?
For since, in the wisdom of God, the world did not know God
through wisdom, it pleased God through the folly of what we preach
to save those who believe.
For Jews demand signs and Greeks seek wisdom,
but we preach Christ crucified, a stumbling block to Jews and folly
to Gentiles,
but to those who are called, both Jews and Greeks, Christ the power
of God and the wisdom of God.
For the folly of God is wiser than men, and the weakness of God is
stronger than men.[136]

The folly of God is the wisdom of the cross, which symbolizes both the
wisdom of love and the human being at the crossroads of the four direc-
tions. This intersection is the incarnation of love in the acts of the One
whose wisdom transmits the "peace which passeth understanding."[137]

In contrast to the wisdom of the sophists and the Pharisees, who
"speak but do not act," Yeshua offers an entirely different wisdom. The

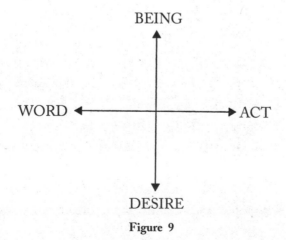

Figure 9

---

[136]1 Cor 1: 19–25.
[137]Phil 4:7.

very desire for it is an expression of Being, and the thought of this Being translates the desire, generating words that are inseparable from acts. This is the fourfold wisdom of the cross, symbolizing the incarnation of all the dimensions of humanity.

The crossroads of these opposites is found in the heart, the abode of the wisdom of love.

In more contemporary schools of thought[138] we can find echoes of this fourfold Wisdom of the cross also expressed as the intersection and integration of human faculties (see figure 10).

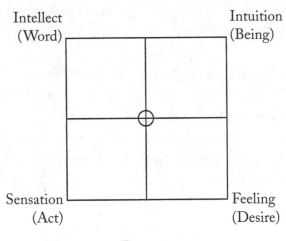

Figure 10

The center here is called the Self. This is the abode of the fully human individual, liberated from all dualism and dispersions, reborn and reharmonized so as to constitute a true Anthropos. The Gospel of Mary is in accord with certain currents of contemporary psychology that define illness in terms of the disharmony of our faculties. Often one or another of our faculties will start to operate independently of the others, very much as if it were contemptuous of them. This discord of our functions is also

---

[138][For example C. G. Jung's fourfold scheme, which is essentially the same as the one given here.—*Trans.*]

an aspect of the climate of wrath. Such fragmentation is ultimately fatal to our health, for each component (feeling, thinking, sensing, intuition) can only perform its true function in harmonious concert with the whole.

It is significant that the Gospel of Mary insists upon this distinction between true wisdom and false, worldly wisdom infected by guile and madness. In some of the earliest Christian communities, Miriam of Magdala herself was considered to be an incarnation of Sophia, she who was destined in both history and metahistory to marry the Logos. But in order to attain this true wisdom, which is the realization of wholeness and maturity, it is necessary to have passed through and overcome the illusory wisdom symbolized by the fifth, sixth, and seventh climates, or demons, that oppress the soul.

> *Yet among the mature we do impart wisdom, though it is not a wisdom of this age or of the rulers of this age, who are doomed to pass away.*
> *But we impart a secret and hidden wisdom of God, which God decreed before the ages for our glorification.*
> *None of the rulers of this age understood this; for if they had, they would not have crucified the Lord of glory.*
> *But, as it is written, "What no eye has seen, nor ear heard, nor the heart of man conceived, what God has prepared for those who love him."*[139]

In these words from Paul, those who do not love God are not only blocked from access to this wisdom, they remain under the influence of wrath, like children who revile and trample upon a gift from someone whom they hate, yet who loves them.

> *"These are the seven manifestations of Wrath,*
> *and they oppressed the soul with questions:*

---

[139]1 Cor 2: 6–9.

'Where do you come from, murderer?'
and 'Where are you going, vagabond?' [140]

The soul that succumbs to these seven demons is thus treated not only as a vagabond whose orientation to the nous and Pneuma has been lost, but as a murderer as well. It would seem that the negation of the noetic-spiritual dimension of humanness is a kind of murder of that which is truly human, leaving the soul with the ability to produce only a grotesque parroting of wisdom, which will ultimately reduce it to a sub-human existence. This is to rob ourselves of what is both best and essential in us: the possibility of a wisdom that is *capax Dei*, "capable of God," of an intimacy with one's Creator.

Might not some modern psychologies create an obstruction to this precious capacity of becoming fully human? Certainly some of them refuse to acknowledge any reality beyond psychic activity fed only by sensory input and memory components of the unconscious. This is often accompanied by a scientific reductionism that equates feelings and thoughts with physiological and neural activity, mistaking the biological support of the psyche for the psyche itself.

Those who object to the term *murdered* as too harsh a description of those of us who experience the effects of such schools of thought will at least have to accept *crippled*, for this is how we are left when we adopt belief systems that literally cut us off from that dimension that enables us to become fully human.

Paul would seem to be in accord with the viewpoint of the Gospel of Mary when he addresses those who are still stuck in a psychic climate dominated by wrath and jealousies of the flesh:

> But my brothers, I could not address you as spiritual men, but
> as men of the flesh, as babes in Christ.
> I fed you with milk, not solid food, for you were not ready for it.

---

[140]The Coptic word *t-ouasf-ma* could also be translated as "wanderer" or "tramp."

And even now you are not ready, for you are still of the flesh.
For while there is still jealousy and strife among you, are you
not still of the flesh, and behaving like ordinary men?[141]

[Page 16, continued]
15   *The soul answered:*
16   *'That which oppressed me has been slain;*
17   *that which encircled me has vanished;*
18   *my craving has faded,*
19   *and I am freed from my ignorance.'"*

The previous interrogation has been a necessary "oppression" in the soul's self-questioning as to its place in the human world and in the universe. After voyaging through the wrathful climates of darkness, craving, ignorance, jealousy, and madness masquerading as wisdom, it finally reaches deliverance and intones its chant of victory:

> *"'That which oppressed me has been slain;*
> *that which encircled me has vanished;*
> *my craving has faded,*
> *and I am freed from my ignorance.'"*

This is the psyche turned toward the nous, and through it toward the Pneuma. It is no longer subject to craving and ignorance, for it has discovered the harmonious order of the human manifold. The soul's spirit can now *rejoin* the Holy Spirit.

It is interesting that Paul also makes this distinction between the merely psychic, mortal man (likened to a murderer or to a dead man himself) and the spiritual man. The latter is like a living Breath, filled with the Spirit (Pneuma) that plumbs all the depths and heights of God. Unlike the

---

[141]1 Cor 3:1–3.

merely psychic man, the spiritual man can be neither judged nor understood by any person. As the Teacher says in Jn 3:7–8: "The wind blows
where it wills, and you hear the sound of it, but you do not know whence it
comes nor where it goes; so it is with every one who is born of the Spirit."

Paul elaborates on this theme in 1 Cor 2:10–15:

> *Indeed the Spirit [Pneuma]*[142] *searches everything, even the*
> *depths of God.*
> *For what person knows a man's thoughts except the Spirit that*
> *is in him? So also no one comprehends the thoughts of God*
> *except the Spirit of God.*
> *Now we have received not the spirit of the world,*[143] *but the*
> *Spirit that is from God,*[144] *that we might understand the gifts*
> *bestowed on us by God.*
> *And we impart this in words not taught by human wisdom,*
> *but taught by the Spirit, interpreting spiritual realities*[145] *to*
> *those who possess the Spirit.*
> *The psychic man*[146] *does not receive the gifts of the Spirit of*
> *God, for they are folly to him, and he is not able to understand*
> *them because they are spiritually discerned.*
> *The spiritual man judges all things, but is himself to be judged*
> *by no one.*

Having become spiritual, the soul of Miriam participates in this
rediscovery of freedom, which is also sovereignty and detachment. When
certain other apostles begin to judge her, they only show that they are still

---

[142]In the Greek text of Paul, it is definitely Pneuma that is meant. Thus the Breath of man and the
Breath of God become one in the kiss *(nasak)* of the nous.

[143]*Pneuma ton kosmon.*

[144]*To Pneuma to ek tou Théou.*

[145]*Pneumatikois, Pneumatika.*

[146][This may seem odd, but is closer to the original Greek than is the usual translation of "unspiritual
man": *psukikos,* as opposed to *pneumatikos.*—Trans.]

captives of the psychic and the fleshly, which ultimately lead only to mortification and mortality.

> *We know that we have passed from death into life, because we*
> *love one another. He that does not love abides in death.*
> *Whoever hates his brother is a murderer: and you know that no*
> *murderer has eternal life abiding in him.*[147]

It is surprising to find in both these words attributed to John and the words in the Gospel of Mary this same theme expressed with the same language. Worldly wisdom is loveless wisdom, ruled by wrath and cunning. It is also murderous, for it is cut off from the Breath of Life in itself. The wisdom (Sophia) of love *(agapé)* is limitless and unconditional. Because it is beyond all boundaries, it cannot be encircled by the objects of its attention. Because it is always larger than its contents, it neither encloses, craves, nor possesses what it loves.

One may well ask at this point: Is a love without craving or self-interested desire really possible for us? Speaking from a purely psychic standpoint, the answer would have to be no. Simple psychological honesty compels us to admit that our psychic experience of love is never totally untainted by self-interested desires, whether conscious or unconscious. We generally love expecting at the very least to be loved in return—though this has not yet reached the point of craving.

It is clear that there can be no psychic love that is free and disinterested. But the love of which we are speaking is of an entirely different desire. This spiritual desire that Miriam embodies is the same love that she encounters in the eyes and on the lips of her rabbuni, Yeshua. As she herself says, "my craving has faded." We might also translate this as "my *desire*," in the merely psychic sense of that word. Yet this does not mean that her desire has been annihilated. Miriam's spirit (nous) has been

---

[147]1 Jn 3:14–15.

awakened to the Spirit of God, but this does not mean she has ceased to be endowed with a soul or psyche as long as she lives in space-time.

What it does mean is that this soul, with all its psychic activity, is at peace. Its transparency no longer obscures the vision of *what is* and therefore of her true relation with what is, which is agapé, or love. She has been delivered from the tension that is always at least subtly present in our loving when we do not unconditionally accept the another's right to be different, to not love us in return, or to leave us. She has been delivered from the ignorance that makes another into an object that we may possess and keep for life, and into that knowledge that sees the other as a subject endowed with inalienable freedom whom one may love for life.

[Page 17]

1   *"I left the world with the aid of another world;*

2   *a design was erased,*

3   *by virtue of a higher design.*

4   *Henceforth I travel toward Repose,*

5   *where time rests in the Eternity of time;*

6   *I go now into Silence.'"*

7   *Having said all this, Mary became silent,*

8   *for it was in silence that the Teacher spoke to her.*

It requires a higher love to free oneself from a lower love. By the same token, it takes a higher and vaster representation of the world to free oneself from a lower one. Scientific progress itself depends on this.

Applying this to anthropologies, it is imperative that we find a less fragmented, more holistic vision of humankind than the ones dominant today if we are to evolve in a positive sense—for the world in which we human beings live is shaped by our own image of ourselves. A better world necessitates a better anthropology.

The Gospel of Mary, along with other gospels, can help us fine-tune our representations of human-ness through the image of the Teacher—a privileged image of the fully human being who is made in the image of God, a Man-God or a God-Man.

"I left the world with the aid of another world;'"

The world of the soul is freed by its opening to the nous-pneuma, revealing another world. To change worlds is to change worldviews. The eyes of the flesh and the eyes of the spirit do not see the same reality.

We noted previously that it is by virtue of her discovery of the imaginal through the awakening of her nous that Miriam is able to move from the material to the spiritual. The imaginal is that in-between zone where spirits become embodied and bodies become spiritualized. It is where the vision of a homogeneous reality (whether a material or a spiritual one) gives way to a vision of multidimensional realms, a hierarchy ranging from the densest to the most subtle realities.

The different phases of Miriam's soul-voyage have enabled us if not to *see* then at least to experience these climates, albeit with our baggage of reserve, enthusiasm, irony, or whatever constitutes our habitual patterns of thought.

For sensory reality, as for historical reality, the distinction of real vs. imaginary tends to boil down to true vs. false. This is not the case for imaginal reality, however. For the imaginal is not merely something that is at best possible, as is the imaginary. Rather, it is of an ontological reality entirely superior to that of mere possibility.[148] Imaginal realities are no less endowed with real Being than are the factual realities that are the basis of history. Furthermore, history itself ceases to exist when it degenerates into a mere collection of facts unconnected by a story—and this story cannot be found without a transcendent dimension that sees these facts from within and beyond.

Those who change history create a fracture in the deterministic story of their era. Like Yeshua, Miriam, and many other founders of great

---

[148]Cf. Jambet, *La Logique des Orientaux*, 211.

spiritual traditions, they are like flashes of lightning in the dark of our ordinary history. They embody what the Greeks called *kairos*, an instant of "the intersection of time and eternity," which introduces the salutary vertical dimension into the horizontality of *chronos*.[149]

> "'. . . *a design was erased,*
> *by virtue of a higher design.*'"

The lower design is that of ordinary time, containing the world and its humanity. As long as this design prevails, the imaginal itself becomes but a moment through which soma, psyche, nous, and Pneuma live out their passage (*pessakh,* in Hebrew—the word also used for the holiday of Passover, and for Easter by the first Christians). Yet:

> "*Henceforth I travel toward Repose,*'"

Thus the fulfillment of a week of work is Shabbat, whose etymological root means "to stop"—to stop doing, producing, thinking, to stop time.

The Anthropos created in the image of YHWH knows true repose and how to savor individual being as Being, free of all need to prove ourselves or to justify our existence through any sort of accomplishment.

The difficulty for the psyche is that this highest climate has no weather! It lacks all the sensations, emotions, thoughts, and even intuitions through which the psyche has become accustomed to feeling its own existence. Even love does not feel like love in this space. Yet here is precisely the test of the soul's authenticity, for this is the space of the very source of love. Is the soul still capable of love here, where it can no longer feel love? To the extent that we are attached to the feeling of being "in love," we lack authenticity of soul, for in reality we love our own pleasur-

---

[149]In Greek myth, Chronos is also the god of time who devours his children.

able emotions (i.e., motion) that we experience through another. But when we truly love another unconditionally, the psyche basks in that climate of repose and has no need to be moved by this love.

As Aristotle so eloquently said, contemplation is the purest of human action. It brings us closest to the original act of the unmoved Mover that sets all worlds into motion yet is itself moved by nothing. Miriam's path now leads toward this purest act, her utterly gratuitous love, which is not other than Being itself. It is here that:

"'. . . time rests in the Eternity of Time;'"

Eternity is the absence of time, and is totally incompatible with conventional religious doctrines of eternal life. In these systems, time is still in fact going on forever—though perhaps at a slower pace—in the sense of continuing to flow without coming to an end. But we can all too easily imagine boredom in such an eternity, and this is precisely why it is bogus.

In order for boredom to even be possible, we must first have a background of *passing time*. But there is no passing time in Eternity. As creatures of passing time, the closest we can come to representing it is through those instants of greatest aliveness and intensity of Presence—and of course any representation of such an instant is bound to be a relative and fleeting image.

The eternal Son of Man in us is also the Son of the Instant, and it is here that Miriam comes, in silence, to experience her wedding with eternity. The repose to which she goes is also silence, as she says in the same breath. Yet this silence is also of the beyond— it cannot be reduced to the popular slogan "here and now," inasmuch as that implies dependence upon experience in passing time.

In ancient traditions, silence was called "the breast of the Father" *(en sigeï: hn noukarōf)*, the transcendence in the heart of immanence. Ignatius of Antioch explicitly states that the Word (Logos) comes from Silence and returns to Silence (symbolized by the Father). Between the Silence of the Source and that of the end, there is a time for word (logos) and breath (pneuma) when human beings are given the possibility—which is also their blessing—of participation and of understanding as much as they can.

Even Clement of Alexandria had some rather strange and beautiful words to say on this:

> Silence, they say, is Mother of all beings born of the Abyss. Inasmuch as she has expressed the inexpressible, she has kept to silence. Inasmuch as she has understood, she has named it: the incomprehensible.[150]

This is part of the great *apophatic* tradition of the early Church Fathers.[151] According to it, YHWH remains incomprehensible, inaccessible. We can only know his names, qualities, reflections (Gregory Palamas called them his "energies"); we can know the Son and the Holy Spirit, but not the inaccessible Essence.

We can only know the radiation of the sun, never its heart, where light is most dense and always hidden to us. Both physicists and mystics speak of the darkness at the core of light. Of course these are only analogies, yet their message is that in the physical domain, as in the spiritual, the essential always eludes our minds. We only come close to it through silence and repose.

Having said all this, Mary became silent

It is vanity to speak too much of the ineffable Silence, even though it is through words that we arrive at it. Beyond a certain point, there is only wordless communion.

for it was in silence that the Teacher spoke to her.

---

[150]Clement of Alexandria, *Excerpts to Theodotus*, 29.

[151]See the author's introductions to Saint John Chrysostom in *Homelie sur l'incompréhensibilité de Dieu* (Paris: Albin Michel), and to Gregory of Nyssa in *La Vie de Moïse* (Paris: Albin Michel).

These meetings between Logos and Sophia reverberate in realms of both words and silences.

> *Happy are those who have ears to hear the Teacher's words;*
> *Happier still are those who have ears to hear his silence.*

Of course there must have been a sharing of words, feelings, and sense experiences, as well as silences, between Yeshua and Miriam. But it was surely silence that began to fill them when they left the talkative company of the other disciples, and walked together of a star-filled evening beside the softly lapping waters of the Sea of Chennereth. Walking, alone together in that silent communion, even the noetic image was left behind, for there was nothing left to see—only that living, overflowing Nothing which, the next morning, in the language of their time, they would refer to as the Father.

[Page 17, continued]
9   *Then Andrew began to speak, and said to his brothers:*
10   *"Tell me, what do you think of these things she has been telling us?*
11   *As for me, I do not believe*
12   *that the Teacher would speak like this.*
13   *These ideas are too different from those we have known."*
14   *And Peter added:*
15   *"How is it possible that the Teacher talked*
16   *in this manner, with a woman,*
17   *about secrets of which we ourselves are ignorant?*
18   *Must we change our customs,*
19   *and listen to this woman?*
20   *Did he really choose her, and prefer her to us?"*

Miriam has ceased speaking. Her silence annoys her critics as much as her words do, for it is a sign of the peace of the One who inhabits her. They cannot accept her story of the voyage of the soul through the different climates, for it seems like ordinary imagination to them. Yet, in spite of themselves, they appear to be intrigued by her teaching about the relation between psyche, nous, and Pneuma and the difference between the merely psychic person, who only hears the word as they do, and the noetic and spiritual person who is also capable of vision.

How could it be that the Teacher led her into realms unknown to them, his beloved disciples? Had they not shared bread, love, travel, and many hardships with Yeshua? It is Peter who is most predictably irritated by Miriam's questions and the answers she claims to have received. This annoyance is mentioned in only one of several gospels that include the theme of Peter's impatience with her and with women in general:

> Peter said:
> "My Lord, can't these women stop asking so many questions
> so that we may ask our own?"
> Jesus said to Mary and the other women:
> "Then let your brothers ask their questions."[152]

But more ominous than the recurrent male/female tensions within the group of disciples is the implication of Andrew's reaction when he questions the validity of her report itself, suggesting that her words are a false teaching:

> "Tell me, what do you think of these things she has been telling
> us?
> As for me, I do not believe
> that the Teacher would speak like this.
> These ideas are too different from those we have known."

---

[152] *Pistis Sophia* 377: 14–17.

As far as he is concerned she has been ranting. In fact, the subtle and complex cosmology implied by her vision is something better addressed to educated folk, not to simple Galilean fishermen. Yeshua had preferred to speak to them in parables—which they generally did not understand either, but at least these left an imprint on the heart, the message of which could emerge later.

As in other gospels, Matthew confirms the importance of this practice of using parables:

> All this Jesus said to the crowds in parables; indeed he said
> nothing to them without a parable.
> This was to fulfil what was spoken by the prophet: "I will open
> my mouth in parables, I will utter what has been hidden since
> the foundation of the world."[153]

The Teacher makes it clear in these passages from the canonical Gospels that these words and images will be interpreted according to the level of consciousness of the person. He also indicates that at least some disciples are capable of deeper understanding beyond the need for parables. Why should Miriam not have been among those privileged disciples to whom he could reveal the hidden meaning of images such as the Kingdom, or the reign of the Spirit (Pneuma) evolving within the Anthropos:

> Then the disciples came and said to him, "Why do you speak to
> them in parables?"
> And he answered them, "To you it has been given to know the
> secrets of the kingdom of heaven, but to them it has not been
> given
> For to him who has will more be given, and he will have
> abundance; but from him who has not, even what he has will
> be taken away.
> This is why I speak to them in parables, because seeing they do

---

[153]Mt 13:34–35. See also Mk 4:33–34.

not see, and hearing they do not hear, nor do they understand.
With them indeed is fulfilled the prophecy of Isaiah which says:
'You shall indeed hear but never understand, and you shall
indeed see but never perceive.
For this people's heart has grown dull, and their ears are heavy
of hearing, and their eyes they have closed, lest they should
perceive with their eyes, and hear with their ears, and
understand with their heart, and turn for me to heal them.'
But blessed are your eyes, for they see, and your ears, for they
hear.
Truly, I say to you, many prophets and righteous men longed to
see what you see, and did not see it, and to hear what you hear,
and did not hear it."[154]

The Teacher's words about giving more to him who has, and taking away from him who has not, may seem harsh and puzzling. There are at least two levels of meaning that must be considered in order to understand this. First, for those who are filled with intelligence and love, all things seem to be given; but for those who lack the love and intelligence needed in order to come into relation with Being, nothing really has savor or meaning, no matter how many possessions they may have.

At another level—perhaps closer to the anthropology of the Gospel of Mary, but also found in the Gospels of Matthew, Mark, and Luke—those who "have not" are those who operate only through gross sensual perception, and who therefore have no access to the Kingdom of the Spirit (Pneuma). They see the world only in its densest aspects and lack any light and subtle perception of its poetic aspect. They have no sense of the "visible surrounded by the invisible," nor of any sort of impalpable dimension of an object they hold in their hands.[155]

Access to the Kingdom requires not only the awakening of the nous,

---

[154]Mt 13:10–17.

[155]See Teilhard de Chardin's experience of the Divine in the *impalpable* aspect of a piece of mineral he was holding in his hand.

but also of those spiritual senses that can put us in contact with that realm *in between* the realm of the physical senses—understood through weight, measure, and analysis—and the world of the *Deus Absconditus*,[156] the purely immaterial, divine world of the clear light.

The Kingdom would seem to correspond to the *mundus imaginalis,* which we mentioned earlier in connection with Corbin. A very special sensitivity, love, and intelligence must be developed in order to perceive this world. The reason given by Yeshua for spiritual blindness and deafness is that the nous,[157] or spirit, has become calloused, and the heart closed. The obstruction of the inner eye means that things can only be seen from the outside. The attention comes to rest and is trapped in their appearances, in their being-for-death.

In the Gospel of Matthew, Yeshua is quite explicit on this subject:

> *The eye is the lamp of the body. So, if your eye is sound, your*
> *whole body will be full of light;*
> *but if your eye is not sound, your whole body will be full of*
> *darkness. If then the light in you is darkness, how great is that*
> *darkness!* [158]

Could it be that the nous of some of the disciples has become closed? Might they not be prey to the climate of darkness evoked in Matthew as well as in the Gospel of Mary?

We must bear in mind that our narrative takes place after the Resurrection. The Teacher has left the world of history and anyone who longs to remain in relationship with him must learn to use unaccustomed organs of perception if they are to apprehend a new world. "It is no longer through the flesh that we shall know the Christ," said Paul of Tarsus.

---

[156] *Deus Absconditus,* "the Hidden God."

[157] In some texts we find the word *kardia* substituted. For the Semites, the heart (and sometimes the spirit) is the source of thoughts. See A. Guillaumont, "Le sens des noms du coeur dans l'antiquité," in *Le Coeur* (Paris: Etudes carmélitaines, 1950), 67–77.

[158] Mt 6:22–23. See also Lk 11:34–35.

The reaction of Andrew and Peter in the Gospel of Mary is an illustration of the climate in which the disciples found themselves after the Resurrection. They experienced emotions of grief and fear, and a refusal to really accept the Good News, especially if it happened to come from women, and particularly from the one known as Miriam of Magdala:

> *Now when he arose from the tomb early on the first day of the*
> *week, he appeared first to Mary Magdalene, from whom he*
> *had cast out seven demons.*
> *She went and told those who had been with him, as they*
> *mourned and wept.*
> *But when they heard that he was alive and had been seen by*
> *her, they would not believe it.*[159]
>
> *Now it was Mary Magdalene and Joanna and Mary the*
> *mother of James and the other women with them who told this*
> *to the apostles;*
> *but these words seemed to them idle rambling, and they did not*
> *believe them.*[160]

Mary's words are, then, the idle ramblings of a woman and therefore are of no interest or importance—each of them could comfortably turn his attention elsewhere. Peter adds:

> *"How is it possible that the Teacher talked*
> *in this manner with a woman*
> *about secrets of which we ourselves are ignorant?*
> *Must we change our customs,*
> *and listen to this woman?*
> *Did he really choose her, and prefer her to us?"*

---

[159]Mk 16:9–11.
[160]Lk 24:10–11.

There can be no doubt that Peter is genuinely shocked that a woman could speak with such authority, revealing secrets that they, Yeshua's closest male disciples, did not know. There are plenty of other early Christian texts dealing with this subject, and several of them make specific mention of Peter's mistrust of women—apparently even including his own daughter!

> Our brother Peter shunned places where women were present. Even more, when there arose a scandal regarding his daughter, he prayed to the Lord, and his daughter became paralyzed on her side, so that no one could lie with her.[161]

There is even a second version of this same event:

> The leader of the apostles, Peter, would flee at the sight of a woman's face. But his daughter was so pretty to look at that a scandal was provoked by her beauty of form, and he started to pray, and she became paralyzed.[162]

Thanks to her father's influence, Petronilla (for such was her name) was able to die "a virgin, a saint, and a martyr."

But not everything is explained by Peter's misogyny. Like Andrew, what really disturbs him is that a woman might know more than he and his men, and might even be able to guide them! For most Jews of that era, this was unthinkable. Like other pious men, Peter thanked God in his prayers each morning for not having made him "invalid, poor, or a woman."

"Must we change our customs?"

Must we grant women a place of equal respect and authority in the

---

[161]Version a, quoted by Tardieu, *Codex de Berlin*, 24.

[162]Acts of Peter, version b, 220.

community? But were women not made to serve men and to satisfy them when asked? For Peter, such customs were not just social, they were religious. The Teacher's behavior with regard to women had always been a puzzle to him. The Samaritan woman, the adulteress, Miriam herself—all these women he had favored with teachings of "prayer in spirit and in truth" (the Samaritan), or "the mercy and forgiveness of the living God" (the adulteress), and finally, the first revelation to Miriam of the Resurrection, the very essence of Christianity itself, as Peter conceived it.

On a more ordinary psychological level, it would seem that the chief of the apostles was simply afraid of women. Wasn't it a woman, a servant who came to warm herself next to him at the fire, who frightened him into denying his master three times, even though he had sworn never to betray the Teacher?[163]

Is it possible to give serious attention to this gospel attributed to a woman, and to dare to learn something of this feminine perspective of the Teacher, without casting doubt on the value of the canonical Gospels?

"Did he really choose her, and prefer her to us?"

Doesn't Jewish scripture also deem it natural for a man to sometimes prefer the company of a woman for intimate sharing? And is this not also a realistic picture of Yeshua's humanity?

But the core of the problem is deeper than this. Before we can become truly spiritual beings, informed and guided by the Pneuma, we must accept ourselves as psychophysical creatures with a soul (psyche) and a body (soma). And this means that the acceptance of our feminine dimensions is absolutely indispensable if we are to have true access to the nous, or for that matter, to the masculine dimensions of our being.

As Karl Graf von Dürkheim remarked, in our age the rediscovery (or discovery) of the spiritual must occur through a reconciliation with the feminine. The goal is the wedding of the masculine and the feminine: the

---

[163]See Mt 26:31–35; Mk 14:27–31; Jn 13:36–38; and his denial in Mt 26:69–75; Mk 14:66–72; and Jn 18:55–58; 25–27.

Anthropos. This wedding must be initiated within us on a social level; on a neurophysiological level (the harmonization of the brain hemispheres); and on a more universal and planetary level. It must be an authentic alliance—without confusion and conflict—of the archetypes of Orient and Occident.

Peter has not yet entered into the climate of the new wedding proposed by the Teacher. The climate of jealousy still holds him back, and his consequent mistrust of the feminine prevents him from reclaiming the missing parts of his love.

[Page 18]

1   *Then Mary wept,*

2   *and answered him:*

3   *"My brother Peter, what can you be thinking?*

4   *Do you believe that this is just my own imagination,*

5   *that I invented this vision?*

6   *Or do you believe that I would lie about our Teacher?"*

Faced with Peter's incomprehension, Miriam's tears are not the ones she knows best—those of grief, love, or awe—but the tears of a child before an adult who refuses to believe her at the very moment when she has most opened her heart in truth.

"My brother Peter, what can you be thinking?"

It is significant that she first addresses him as a brother and friend. One of the practices that the Teacher enjoined upon his disciples was to treat each other as brothers and sisters, with no institution of spiritual hierarchy among them. Indeed, it is this very atmosphere of fellowship in love that makes them recognizable as his disciples. Miriam is thus not addressing Peter as a superior, certainly not as some sort of bishop or pope, but as a brother who has wounded her through his misunderstanding.

Clearly Peter is "in his head" rather than "in his heart." And the thoughts circulating there are those of doubt and suspicion rather than discrimination. And what is happening in his heart? Jealousy and perhaps even contempt are stirring—in any case, certainly not that willing suspension of disbelief that enables us to listen to words we may not always agree with, but that we at least can try to understand.

> *"Do you believe that this is just my own imagination,*
> *that I invented this vision?"*

Here Miriam implicitly affirms the imaginal, transpersonal nature of this vision. It is not merely a "personal" affair. In fact, at least two persons are required: the one who allows herself to be seen, and the one who sees. The personal imagination can of course produce all kinds of colorful representations, but these do not have the power and *presence* of that which is given through the awakened nous, the fine point of Miriam's soul.

We do not invent this reality, we *see* it. Of course we see it in forms accessible to us, hence it cannot be the totality of the Real. And yet it *is* the Real, just as a ray of the sun is not the entire sun, and yet it *is* the sun.

For Andrew and Peter, the temptation is to label Miriam's account as mere personal storytelling. And they already know how to judge such stories, using good sense and reason. But these are insufficient for understanding the *meta*-story, the epiphany of a world and awareness that is "other," of an "Other-Than-Being"[164] in the very core of her story. Beyond sense and reason, this requires an opening of the doors of perception, the awakening of nous, which can then allow the entrance of the Pneuma, or Holy Spirit, also known in Christian discourse as the Consoler, the *consolus*, meaning "that which is with the one who is alone."

Miriam is not simply alone with her personal imagination. She is visited by the living spirit of him who told his disciples in John 16, and in the last verse of Matthew, that he would always be with them. This spirit re-activates the images in her psyche in such a way that they are no longer

---

[164]To borrow a term from the title of a beautiful book by Emmanuel Lévinas, *Autrement qu'Etre*. In some of his reflections, Lévinas is not far from our subject.

just memories. They are vehicles of the real Presence of the Teacher, the Anthropos, Son of Man and of God.

One might say that the Holy Spirit brings about a kind of transubstantiation of the image of the Teacher, so that it becomes truly alive, resurrected within her. This may be accompanied by certain phenomena that mere memory or imagination cannot produce, such as manifestations of light and heat; but above all it is accompanied by peace, patience, confidence, and love.

It is worth noting that in the Orthodox Christian tradition, the Epiclesis is a time when one prays that the Holy Spirit may "descend upon us and upon these offerings" of bread and wine, so that they may become transformed into the "flesh and blood," which also means the action and contemplation, of the living Christ in our midst. In a sense, Miriam has lived this Epiclesis, for the Holy Spirit has informed her mind and heart (nous, kardia) in such a way that the Teacher is now truly seen by her and continues to guide her.

This world of the imaginal is just as real as visible reality, and also just as real as invisible Reality; yet as we have said, it is neither visible nor invisible. In the West it is too easily associated with fantasy, in part because of the resemblance to the word *imagination*. Yet the imaginal is the opening of physical space-time into a different and vaster dimension of time and space. It is not the ultimate Eternity of the Uncreated, yet it leads us there, recalling Jacob's ladder as a symbol of different levels of Being.

The deepest hurt for Miriam is that Peter would think that she is lying. For a Semite, to lie is far worse than to be deluded. It is an act of ill will and an attack upon the Real. As Meister Eckhart said at his trial in Avignon, "I may be wrong, but I cannot lie."

But even worse for her is the implication that the Resurrection itself could be seen as a lie. By indulging in his suspicions, Peter risks losing his own faith and trust in a love that transcends the grave. Instead of strengthening his brothers, he risks weakening them with factionalism and dragging them back down into the world of death from which the Teacher came to liberate them.

Thus it is also the very Christ in her that is wounded and moved by this reaction, crucified once more by his own disciples and friends—in this case, rebuked by his especially beloved hardheaded friend, his *kepha* (rock), Peter. Instead of becoming the rock on which the community is built, Peter is throwing stones.

[Page 18, continued]

7 *At this, Levi spoke up:*

8 *"Peter, you have always been hot-tempered,*

9 *and now we see you repudiating a woman,*

10 *just as our adversaries do.*

11 *Yet if the Teacher held her worthy,*

12 *who are you to reject her?*

13 *Surely the Teacher knew her very well,*

14 *for he loved her more than us.*

Levi is already known to us from the synoptic Gospels:

> *He went out again beside the sea; and all the crowd gathered about him, and he taught them.*
>
> *And as he passed on, he saw Levi the son of Alphaeus sitting at the tax office, and he said to him, "Follow me." And Levi rose and followed him.*[165]

It is this man of spontaneity, ready to leave everything to walk *(acolouthaï)* with Yeshua, who reproaches Peter for attacking *(gumnazesthai)* Miriam.

Peter is behaving more like an adversary than a brother or friend. He has forgotten the Teacher's counsel to "love one another, as I have loved you." Their adversaries, whether called Pharisees, Essenes, Romans, or

---

[165]Mk 2:13–14.

others, are those who do not respect the right of women to study religion, much less to teach it. Yet "if the Teacher held her worthy," granting her the capacity to love and understand him, then who is Peter to oppose this? Levi is clearly aware of Peter's reputation as a proud, hot-tempered man *(tó orgilou):*

> *From that time Jesus began to show his disciples that he must go to Jerusalem and suffer many things from the elders and chief priests and scribes, and be killed, and on the third day be resurrected.*
> *And Peter took him and began to reprimand him, saying, "God forbid, Lord! This shall never happen to you."*
> *But he turned and said to Peter, "Get behind me, Satan! You are a hindrance to me; for you are not on the side of God, but of men."*[166]

This is the same disposition that impelled Peter to draw his sword and cut off the ear of the high priest's servant (Jn 18:10); and later to swear vehemently, and even curse, in his denial of any association with Jesus (Mt 26:74). But in spite of his reputation of pride and misogyny, widely attested in early Christian literature, Peter's character had another, very different side: He was a very generous man, capable of great sincerity and spontaneity, and he was said to have been the first to recognize the Son of God in the Son of Man (Mt 16:16). Yet here also Yeshua implies that Peter's insight does not come from the psyche, but from the nous— that is, through the revelation of the Holy Spirit. If Peter had not been open to this, his habitual psychology would have prevailed, and if indulged indefinitely, he might have even become a *shatan,* an obstruction to vision and to the divine plan: Walk forth, Simon Bar-Jona! For flesh and blood has not revealed this to you, but my Father who is in heaven.[167]

---

[166]Mt 16:21–23.
[167]Mt 16:17.

There is a curious parallel between Peter's attitude toward Miriam and his attitude toward Yeshua himself. At first Peter, inspired by his own openness, treats her with great respect, asking her to reveal unknown teachings; and then he shuts down, rejecting her account of Yeshua as women's nonsense. This is a good illustration of the duality that is ubiquitous in ordinary humanity—the continual opening and closing of the psyche toward the Pneuma.

But Levi reminds him that he has no right to reject that which he does not understand. Who does he think he is, a lawmaker? The validity of Miriam's vision is strictly an affair between her and God.

This recalls an incident in the life of Pope John XXIII when he was overcome by worry and sadness regarding the future of the Church. In a vision, the Christ appeared to him, and said, "Is it you or I who is responsible for the Church of Churches? Who do you think you are?" Indeed, who do we think we are, to reject and excommunicate each other? We can trust in Being to know the heart of its beings, just as the Teacher knew the heart of Miriam.

Finally, Levi reminds Peter of what he himself had recognized earlier: the special love of Yeshua for Miriam of Magdala.

"The last shall be first . . . the tax-collectors and prostitutes will enter the Kingdom before you." This is one of the most famous gospel texts, beautifully illustrated by Dostoyevsky's scene in which Christ invites thieves and other disreputable men and women to a great feast in celebration of the Kingdom. Why is it that such people are said to precede us into the Kingdom? Simply because they do not consider themselves worthy.

We are not to judge ourselves. Only the love that moves the Earth, the stars, and the human heart can judge us. The Teacher is like a spring that offers water to all who are thirsty. It is not the light that fails us, it is our eyes that fail the light. It is not water that is wanting, it is thirst. It is desire.

Miriam is the woman of desire, which includes all desires, from those of the flesh to those of the highest reaches of soul, mind, and Spirit. She is the holy bride who unites with her Beloved to say to all: "Come!"

The Spirit and the Bride say: "Come!" Let all who hear say:
"Come!" May all who thirst drink freely of the Water of Life.[168]

Our blankness shall give way to Being, and our absurdity to grace—
gratuitously.

Like the other Mary, she is indeed full of grace.

> **[Page 18, continued]**
> 15   *Therefore let us atone,*
> 16   *and become fully human [Anthropos],*
> 17. *so that the Teacher can take root in us.*
> 18   *Let us grow as he demanded of us,*
> 19   *and walk forth to spread the gospel,*
> 20   *without trying to lay down any rules and laws*
> 21   *other than those he witnessed."*

There was once a nun who came to visit Abba Anthony, one of the
most celebrated of the desert fathers. When a young monk noticed her
among the assembled brothers, he was deeply shocked, and demanded to
know why a woman was allowed in their remote desert monastery. Abba
Anthony anwered: "Look well among all us monks assembled here, and
you will see only one human being—her."

Like Levi, and unlike Andrew and Peter, Anthony was speaking of
the Anthropos, which he recognized in this woman. The male-female
alliance here also echoes the couple of Yeshua and Miriam, symbolizing
the dual teaching of Sophia (wisdom, creative imaginal vision, silence)
and Logos (wisdom, creative teaching and words, silence).

"Therefore let us atone" was also what Yeshua taught when he selected
his first disciples. They were enjoined to convert or repent in the original
sense of *teshuva*, "to return"—to return to ourselves, our true center.
Repentance in this sense is the return from what is contrary to one's nature

---

[168]Rv 22:17.

to what is true to it. This is the meaning of the Greek word *metanoia*, beyond the nous—in its sense of mind limited by ordinary thought—and toward Pneuma—the Holy Spirit, Breath, and Living Light.

Having turned away from the "old man"[169] and his conscious and unconscious memories and programming, we can now enter the way of the new man, also known as the perfect man, or the "man in relation with his finality" *(endusáménoì tón téleion anthropón)*. These expressions were also used by Paul of Tarsus.[170]

Thus the Anthropos that the Gospel of Mary is preparing us to assume is also our *telòs*, the goal of our existence. Henri Bergson once said that the universe is "a machine for making gods." But it would be truer to say that the universe is a creative imagination and process that demands both human and god. The two become One in the full realization of the Anthropos, the Christos Yeshua, Son of Man and Son of God.

". . . so that the Teacher can take root in us."

If we allow him to arise in the heart of our life, growing and taking root in us, we will be guided by his Spirit toward our wholeness and fulfillment. This is how we have always been dreamed, imagined, and created by Being. Yet we are free to obstruct this process of becoming, for it is only in freedom that it can take place. There is no predestination in this growth of the Teacher within us—our tree of life must be free in order to grow toward its light.

This dream is very real, and this creative imagination is very powerful. What is required of us is that we give to all of our actions and encounters their full savor, meaning, and intensity of love. To allow the Anthropos to take root and flourish within us is to continue unceasingly to introduce into all our actions, even the most banal and everyday, just a

---

[169][Curiously, the Germanic etymology of the English word *world* is literally *wer-aldh* , which means "old man."—*Trans.*]

[170]See Gal 3:27; and Col 1:28.

little more consciousness and love. We must imagine and believe that it is this that will at least make the world liveable, if not save it.

This is what the Teacher has asked of us: to "walk forth," and share this Good News (gospel, euangelion). A human being is not a beast, or a computer, or a mere passing phenomenon, doomed to die. A human being is designed for anastasis—resurrection—in the sense that Yeshua manifests and teaches it, and as Miriam contemplates it in this gospel.

"... *without trying to lay down any rules and laws other than those he witnessed.*"

There is nothing to be added, but much to be lived. We must allow Life to live within us, so as to join him in witnessing the divine vitality that drives a human being to bloom and exude the perfume of God.

Like her Beloved, Miriam of Magdala holds nothing back of this perfume, nor of the radiance of her flowering. Even today, her image is still surrounded by its richly colored aura. For those who have eyes to see, as well as ears to hear, the world is still being illumined by the brilliance of Yeshua and Miriam.

[Page 19]

1 *When Levi had said these words,*

2 *they all went forth to spread the gospel.*

3 *THE GOSPEL*
   ACCORDING TO
   MARY

After this brief and cogent reminder by Levi, there is nothing more to discuss. Further understanding must now come through action, and the disciples are well aware of the echoes of the Teacher's "Walk forth!" in Levi's words.

These words have a special resonance twenty centuries later. The original sense of action (missing in the narrow rendering of the Beatitudes as "Blessed are . . .") is restored. It invites us to stop indulging in complacent satisfaction, even in areas where we think nothing more is to be done. There is no finality in this process of humility, for we can always do more, and go further—as the pilgrims of Compostela said, inspired by those of Emmaus before them: *Ultreia!*[171] There is another step still further beyond the limitations of the known and the habitual, which we are always taking to be the Real.

". . . they all went forth to spread the gospel."

They will witness and live the Good News. This is a permanent challenge, and not one to be met by mere proselytizing.

At this turn of the millennium there are many who balk at the endlessness of the imperative to keep going beyond. Pessimism is a powerful temptation, as is the pseudo-wisdom of "nothing new under the sun," or "business as usual." But there will be no more business at all if we destroy ourselves, and perhaps even the planetary ecosystem.

This new threat under which we live has led many to espouse a life of enjoyment of the moment. But without any support of the vertical dimension, this enjoyment turns out to be hollow. How much longer can people continue to use the word *happiness* for the vacuous trances of consumer bliss and petty power that they try to take from a world that is a psychic, intellectual, and spiritual wasteland?

Among Christian writings, the Gospel of Mary is especially cogent as a reminder of the vastness of human potential and of the meaning, beauty, and demands of the human enterprise. It affirms that a human being can only be fulfilled by overcoming herself or himself, going beyond the conditioning of masculine or feminine, so as to become Anthropos—both *anthropocosmos* and *theanthropos*.

---

[171]This was a watchword of encouragement among the pilgrims, meaning "still more," or "further beyond."

But might this not be too grandiose? Is this not a form of utopianism or even megalomania? Some would say so, and this may have something to do with the fact that this gospel, like that of Thomas, had to wait, buried in the sands for almost two thousand years—and then had to wait for decades more, reserved and known only to specialists, before finally beginning to be properly appreciated by a wide public toward the closing years of the twentieth century.

What might be the significance in this timing? Some would say that the Gospel of Mary is the missing piece that has been needed to complete the Good News in a more ecumenical sense, one that would also include and fulfill the Torah and the Qur'an. Yet the important thing is that it invites us to go even further than this, beyond the dualisms and dogmas of all organized religions. It is in this sense that we might well ask ourselves if this is not the appropriate gospel to inaugurate the third millennium.

Yet the present translator and exegete of this gospel would be the first to admit that it is easy to overlook the demands it makes of us. This Anthropos of which the Teacher speaks is not some dream or ideal, it is an intensity of life that wants to be born in us and radiate to the world its intelligence and love. This cannot happen if we do not allow the creative imagination to work in ourselves. Yet is there any other way for us?

The Gospel of Mary Magdalene need not be set up in opposition to other gospels or sacred scriptures, or against recent anthropological or scientific research. If the climate of fragmentation and competition of the vast multitude of contemporary worldviews may be likened to a grim and tense expression upon a human face, then the word of the Teacher in this gospel is like the hint of a smile appearing there—a subtly feminine smile. No doubt this smile comes from the psyche, but its eyes are open windows to the spirit (nous) and to a lucid vision of our possible futures.

In this word there can be felt a Breath (Pneuma) that is surely familiar to us. Perhaps we encountered it in a great wind that came through our life, or perhaps, like Miriam in the Gospel of Philip, in a kiss. There is no conclusion, no finality to the realization of this Spirit, for there is always more to learn in living and breathing more fully the totality of our human potential.

It is this Breath that fills us with the vitality needed to walk forth—not toward our inevitable death, but toward that silent repose in the midst of action, where individual being is finally open to the Oneness of Lover and Beloved.

❧

*THE GOSPEL
ACCORDING TO
MARY*

Cap-Rousset, May 16, 1996

Ascension Day

BIBLIOGRAPHY

Allberry, C. R. C. *A Manichaean Psalmbook*, II. Stuttgart: W. Kohlhammer, 1938.

Bianchi, U. "Docetism: A Peculiar Theory about the Ambivalence of the Presence of the Divine." In *Myths and Symbols: Studies in Honour of Mircea Éliade*. Chicago: University of Chicago Press, 1969.

Blass, F. and A. Debrunner. *A Greek Grammar of the New Testament and Other Early Christian Literature*. Translated and revised by R. W. Funk. Cambridge and Chicago: University of Chicago Press, 1961.

Collins, J. J. "Introduction: Towards the Morphology of a Genre." In *Apocalypse: The Morphology of a Genre, Semeia* 14. Missoula, Mont.: Scholars Press, 1979.

Daniélou, Jean. *The Theology of Jewish Christianity*. Edited and Translated by John A. Baker. London: Darton, Longman, and Todd, 1964.

Dibelius, Martin. *James: A Commentary on the Epistle of James*. Revised by Heinrich Greeven. Translated by Michael A. Williams. Edited by Helmut Koester. Philadelphia: Fortress Press, 1976.

Fallon, F. T. "The Gnostic Apocalypses." In *Apocalypse: The Morphology of a Genre, Semeia* 14. Missoula, Mont.: Scholars Press, 1979.

Finegan, J. *Hidden Records of the Life of Jesus*. Philadelphia and Boston: Pilgrim Press, 1969.

Grant, R. M., ed. *Gnosticism: A Source Book.* New York: Harper, 1961.

Long, H. S. *Diogenis Laertii: Vitae Philosophorum.* Book 7. Oxford, 1964.

MacDermot, Violet. *The Fall of Sophia: A Gnostic Text on the Redemption of Universal Consciousness.* Great Barrington, Mass.: Lindisfarne Books, 2001.

Ménard, J. É. *L'Évangile selon Philippe: Introduction, texte, traduction et commentaire.* Strasbourg, 1967.

———. *L'Évangile selon Thomas.* (NHS, 5). Leiden: E. J. Brill, 1975.

———. *La Lettre de Pierre à Philippe.* Québec: Presses de l'Université Laval, 1977.

Pagels, Elaine. "Visions, Appearances, and Apostolic Authority: Gnostic and Orthodox Traditions." In *Gnosis: Festchrift für Hans Jonas.* Edited by B. Aland. Göttingen, 1978.

———. *The Gnostic Gospels.* New York: Random House, 1980.

Pasquier, A. "L'Eschatologie dans l'Évangile selon Marie: Étude des notions de nature et d'image." In *Colloque international sur les textes de Nag-Hammadi.* Québec and Louvain: 1981.

Perkins, Pheme. *The Gnostic Dialogue: The Early Church and the Crisis of Gnosticism.* New York: Paulist Press, 1980.

Puech, Henri-Charles. "Gnostic Gospels and Related Documents." In *New Testament Apocrypha.* Edited by E. Hennecke and W. Schneemelcher. Philadelphia: Westminster Press, 1963.

Roberts, Colin H. *Catalogue of the Greek and Latin Papyri in the John Rylands Library.* Manchester: Manchester University Press, 1938.

Schmidt, Carl. *Pistis Sophia.* Edited and translated by Violet MacDermot. Leiden: E. J. Brill, 1978.

Schneemelcher, Wilhelm, ed. and R. McL. Wilson, trans. *New Testament Apocrypha.* Rev. ed. Cambridge, England: J. Clarke and Co., 1991–1992.

Tardieu, M. *Trois Mythes gnostiques, Adam, Éros et les animaux d'Égypte dans un écrit de Nag-Hammadi.* Paris, 1974.

Wilson, R. McL. *Gnosis and the New Testament.* Oxford: Blackwell, 1968.

Wilson. R. McL. and G. W. MacRae. "The Gospel According to Mary." In *Nag-Hammadi Library in English.* Edited by James M. Robinson. San Francisco: Harper and Row, 1988.

———. "The Gospel According to Mary." In *Nag-Hammadi Codices V, 2–5 and VI with Papyrus Berolinensis 8502, 1 and 4.* Edited by Douglas M. Parrott. Leiden E. J. Brill, 1979.

van Winden, J. C. M. *An Early Christian Philosopher.* Leiden: E. J. Brill, 1971.

BOOKS OF RELATED INTEREST

The Gospel of Thomas
The Gnostic Wisdom of Jesus
by Jean-Yves Leloup

The Gospel of Philip
Jesus, Mary Magdalene, and the Gnosis of Sacred Union
by Jean-Yves Leloup

The Sacred Embrace of Jesus and Mary
The Sexual Mystery at the Heart of the Christian Tradition
by Jean-Yves Leloup

The Healing Wisdom of Mary Magdalene
Esoteric Secrets of the Fourth Gospel
by Jack Angelo

The Woman with the Alabaster Jar
Mary Magdalen and the Holy Grail
by Margaret Starbird

Mary Magdalene, Bride in Exile
by Margaret Starbird

Return of the Divine Sophia
Healing the Earth through the Lost
Wisdom Teachings of Jesus, Isis, and Mary Magdalene
by Tricia McCannon

Magdalene Mysteries
The Left-Hand Path of the Feminine Christ
by Seren Bertrand and Azra Bertrand, M.D.

Inner Traditions • Bear & Company
P.O. Box 388
Rochester, VT 05767
1-800-246-8648
www.InnerTraditions.com

Or contact your local bookseller